GLOBAL EMPOWERMENT

EMERGING PRACTICES

Uma Narula

ATLANTIC
PUBLISHERS & DISTRIBUTORS (P) LTD

Published by
ATLANTIC
PUBLISHERS & DISTRIBUTORS (P) LTD
B-2, Vishal Enclave, Opp. Rajouri Garden,
New Delhi-110027
Phones : +91-11-25413460, 25429987, 25466842

Sales Office
7/22, Ansari Road, Darya Ganj,
New Delhi-110002
Phones : +91-11-23273880, 23275880, 23280451
Fax : +91-11-23285873
web : www.atlanticbooks.com
E-mail : info@atlanticbooks.com

Branch Office
5, Nallathambi Street, Wallajah Road,
Chennai-600002
Phones : +91-44-64611085, 32413319
E-mail : chennai@atlanticbooks.com

Printed in India
at Nice Printing Press, Ghaziabad, U.P.

Dedicated to

Atul Soni

Who has embarked on a new journey in life to

Understand global empowerment

and

To the younger generation

Who takes tiny steps, then bigger and bigger steps
On the road to global empowerment

Preface

Globalization process creates varied practices in diversified domains of life such as social, political, cultural, economic, entrepreneurial and technological. These practices are based on collective and cumulative experiences of international community and become successively stronger, widely applicable and more effective. These tend to be different from local practices. Such changes will have visible bearing and long-term impact on our (multi-countries') attitudes and behavior, decision-making and leadership, capacity-building and innovations of products and services, and governance, administrative planning and policies in these multi-domains.

What is being practiced, how it is being practiced, and to what context it is being practiced is important; but what is most significant is how it is communicated to players in the global process. The dominant and significant players are: government and political leadership, businesses, civil society, NGOs and people. Changing best practices empower people in diverse domains which in turn create global empowerment. Moreover, practices in the global contexts, if communicated effectively, also create global empowerment.

The world grid is created by international community for social, political, technological, economic and business practices, structures and functions. International community is concerned about happenings in these areas around the world since these have impact on their activities.

We observe that changing emerging practices in globalization of technology, finances and enterprises are creating global empowerment. Hence, the focus of the book *Global Empowerment: Emerging Practices* is on emerging practices in technology, business enterprises, finances and investments. It is important that these emerging practices should be administered effectively for global empowerment; hence, the focus is on public administration domain, viz. decision-making.

The global events as well as the events in India inspired me to think globally and pen those thoughts. The dreams and aspirations, the hopes and despairs, fears and anxieties of people around me goaded me to think globally. The media highlighted these and created the background—the food for thought and the urge to write about.

Organization of book

The book focuses on Emerging Communication Practices in three contexts—globulation, glocalization and globalism—where new practices emerge continuously. Such practices are search for best practices to deliver the products, ideas and services to the majority of the people in a country, in many countries and within the global framework to create global empowerment.

Prologue discusses the need for emerging practices and the growth of healthy communication channels. Chapter 2 "Thinking Global" focuses on globalization communication cycles, globalization perspectives and globalization convergence. It is the integration of technology and flow of information and capital across national borders that are creating a single global marketplace and society.

In Chapter 3 "Communication Technologies: Bridges" the author discusses how technologies are bridges for gaps between existing practices and the innovations, haves and have-nots and how the 'technology bridges' facilitate development and global empowerment through flow and sharing of information. Technology has given promise for the effective progress of businesses and people's lifestyles.

Chapter 4 "Enterprises, Markets: Globalization Contexts" presumes that global empowerment is through enterprises and markets in different parts of the world separately and in conjunction with others, integrating and collaborating. This relates to capital, products and services, productivity and technology and human resources.

Chapter 5 "Creating Enterprises" focuses on two different modes of creating global enterprises—through outsourcing of products and services and using advertising concepts, modes and applications. New outsourcing and advertising practices have emerged that have to be presented differently to a global audience.

Managing enterprises is also important. Chapter 6 "Managing Enterprises, Markets: Emerging Practices" discusses the emerging practices to manage the enterprises and markets. Competition and innovations are important for managing business enterprises in globalization contexts. The flow of funds globally, flow of talents and skills globally, and flow of businesses globally not only interconnect economy but also boost economy worldwide. The significance lies in thinking globally and coping with global trends by capacity-building and improved management techniques and facing changing challenges.

Chapter 7 "Decision-Making: Globalization" discusses how the decision-making practices have changed for participating in globalization and its related issues. Timely and right kind of decision-making is implied for global empowerment.

Epilogue highlights our observations through the chapters about what kind of emerging practices create global empowerment. The key advantage for upstart global contenders is access to some of the world's most dynamic growth markets and immense pool of low-cost resources such as production workers, engineers, land, and petroleum or iron ore. But over and above, the low cost factors are their innovativeness, expertly running businesses, cleverly and perceptively absorbing global consumer trends and technologies and getting new products to markets faster than their rivals.

The best of emerging multinationals though have amassed cash. They have also built global research and development networks and have world-class management. However, we need to make wider applications of technology networks and management principles to draw maximum benefit out of globalization processes.

The book is a focused study of emerging practices in global empowerment. The major concepts in all the related fields have been explained in simple language and lucid manner. Appendices, Bibliography and Subject Index further enrich the book. It will prove immensely useful to the students and teachers of Business Management, Economics and Communication and researchers in these fields.

My acknowledgements are due to my professional colleagues, family and friends for formal discussions about global emerging practices impacting their lifestyles and enterprises.

I am highly thankful to the Chairman, Atlantic Publishers & Distributors (P) Ltd. for his cooperation in bringing out this book.

UMA NARULA

Contents

PART – I

1. Prologue: Emerging Practices
2. Thinking Global
3. Communication Technologies: Bridges

Prologue: Emerging Practices

1

In today's globalization system, it does not matter where you are, and who you are, but what matters the most is what you are, and on that depends the choices you make for prosperity in this system.

Emerging Communication Practices

Many countries are moving towards globalization—the utopian One World. We assume that whosoever does not participate or lags in this race; not only misses the effects of globalization but is bypassed by mainstream world politics, economic, business, technology and cultural influences. The demands of globalization aptly called globulation, that is, the global markets will force upon us the business practices and disciplines which we cannot generate internally. It will make us change many of the practices to fit in these changing scenarios. On the second count, in the domestic scenario, many of the old practices become redundant; new glocalized practices emerge to fit the changing scenario. The glocalization suggest adoption and influence of local cultural practices, local talents and also localizing the global trends. Since divergent values and norms merge as many countries and ethnic cultural groups interact both personally and through media; globalism occurs which suggests a global culture of standardization of food, clothes, music, TV, films, and business styles. Thus, many new practices emerge and we endeavor to communicate our willingness to be in the globalization race through practicing them.

The book focuses on Emerging Communication Practices in these above-mentioned three contexts of globulation, glocalization, and globalism; where new practices emerge continuously. Such practices are search for best practices to deliver the products, ideas and services to the majority of the people in a country, in many countries and within the globalization framework. These Emerging Communication Practices seek to empower people in various domains of life style, business, finances, professions on one hand and on the other empower the political leadership, government and administration of particular country to deal with changing scenarios. Together, we expect global empowerment of people, businesses and governments, since all being in the interdependency loop.

In the early decades of 80s, when we were thinking about the have and have-nots we have been thinking about the economic gaps, social gaps and the gap in the minimum basic needs fulfillment. That led us to our concerns about people's survival, poverty reduction, providing employment and education, and structural reforms of the society. We thought such efforts would develop people and societies and that is how nations will develop. Nations thus developing would empower their people.

Since late 80s decade, the world scenario gradually started changing in many directions due to fast developing technologies of telecommunications led by cellular technologies, and computers; Internet in its various functionalities being the foremost; and the convergence of these and other upcoming technologies. These were connecting people worldwide and were also being shared worldwide both in functionalities and innovations.

People and governments around the world developed different perspectives towards lifestyle, business, finances, professions political leadership, government and administration of a particular country or countries. The interconnectivity of the people facilitated it. These emerging perspectives made people and countries think about global interdependency loop and being in that loop at one point of time or the other. They also sought empowerment through the global interdependency loop since interdependency in this loop was not being dependent by one country on the other but mutual dependency of developed and developing nations, developed or emerging markets on the basis of mutual strengths.

Now there was more talks about things happening in global contexts such as global issues, discussions and solutions suggested; global business collaboration and coordination, decision-making, investments and finances; and over and above technology innovations developed and shared worldwide by one and all. These were the emerging concerns and many emerging communication practices were coming up to deal with these through mutual strengths. This scenario has developed optimally and beneficially in the last twenty-five years; promising more stability, more innovation and therefore constant search for Best, Next and Emerging Communication Practices to bind us all in the global interdependency loop of people, societies, cultures and businesses. In such scenario what will empower people most will be the democracy of communications around the world.

The book further focuses on the emerging communication practices and how change-over has empowered leaders, people, government, NGOs globally in different domains of life through the best practices. We look for best practices of the time and the next practices and the impact of such changeovers.

Best Communication Practices

Practitioners look for practices that could convey to the people what they intend. These communication practices could be the best practices in order to be effective communication. Best practice is a relative term. It depends on people's threshold to understand the message, i.e. the way it is conveyed—its semantic, language, and overall relevancy for comprehensibility and source credibility; and the reach and the accessibility of the channels through which it is conveyed. If the 'effect' of the message is as intended then it is labeled as good practice. Out of a group of good practices, the best practice may be chosen which is most effective. Therefore, a best communication practice is specific to domain, society and segment of society. It is time bound. What is today best may not be the best because of ongoing changes in these variables. So we look for rather next effective practice.

We talk about best practices and pick our practices. Prahlad (2004 b, c) argues that if everyone follows every one's best practice then we converge to meet and the best practice would not give you any advantage. We should rather talk about the next practice. Strategy should always be about the next practice. For example, 20 years back the next practice for businesses was about local responsiveness and global integration. Ten years back it was core competencies and now bottom-of-the-pyramid can be the next practice. There is some intellectual continuity in the three practices: a global company needs to leverage its global strength to bring technology and resources to bear. But it has to be very local; for example, McDonald selling veggie burgers in India and not beef burgers. Businesses enhanced core competencies ten years back to produce focused products. Now they are fast realizing bottom-of-the-pyramid is substantial and cannot be ignored. Only it needs different business models and marketing strategies.

The organized and structured domains for communication practices cover politics, social and economic structures and functions, health, development, urbanization, rural development, business, digital divide, i.e. the use and reach of communication channels. These suggest social practices, ICTs practices, business practices, and political communication practices. Since the practitioners' intended messages aim at positive outcomes; so they look for pragmatic communication practices which have positive and desired effects and intended outcomes; as well as being acceptable to the targeted audience. Many times, they may have to develop another set of sub-practices to persuade the audience to accept the 'main best communication practice'; since practitioners' assume that is the best in their interests. Initially, audience may be unwilling to accept the best practice. Therefore, evaluation of sub-practices at various stages becomes necessary and important for the acceptance of best practices. Some of these best practices are either totally or incrementally innovative, or borrowed, or adaptive according to the lessons learnt.

In the unorganized structures and functions in the above selected domains, the individuals and the groups identify and look for best practice for effective communication when they interact among groups and individuals in different communication contexts and environment. The objective of their best practice is mutual understanding about the communication. In such interpersonal communications, they follow the nuances and twists of conversations and the feedback loops for divergence and convergence to the message. Whatever works for them is the best practice to communicate with one another.

In the 19th and 20th centuries the voice of the West dominated discussions and flow of history. But in 21st century, the civilizations that have been dormant and stagnant are becoming active. We need changing mind-set to accept the challenges of facing the new and diverse world. The need is to bring about integrated cycle of democracy and development. For example, in India the political system allows smooth change over in governments and providing for smooth entry and exit of the political figures without shaking the society. India and its neighbors have a shared destiny. India's prosperity will be their prosperity and their progress will be India's progress. There is mutual interdependency to compete for global economy. Asian countries can fail to become major global economies in the 21st century, if they fail to show the resolve and maturity to grasp the opportunity at hand.

Changing communication practices in selected domains of politics — governance and administration; in social domains of health, development, urbanization, rural development; and of business practices are compared with the earlier existing practices in the same domain or none-existing. We have few assumptions and observations: the democratization of information, technology, finances and investments, leadership and decision-making are affecting the current globalization process and impacting people's lifestyles, businesses and economy. Impacts of communication practices in the particular domain are impacting society, attitudinal and behavioral changes, capacity building and strengthening, economic and political choices. The support mechanisms for practices in these domains are through people, government, NGOs, and international community. The social, business and political communication practices are thus integrated to empower people, institutions and through them the government. For example, in India the social practice of getting equity to disadvantaged groups of people in society through reservation quota (2006) for higher education in medical and technology should not suffocate creativity, merit and enterprise. Groups of people are unhappy, frustrated and disillusioned about the reservation quota policy; and there are countrywide work strikes by doctors and technology students who would be affected most. The political practices need to encourage both in the right perspective to empower people in the true sense.

These changing practices communicated in the right perspective would empower people, government, NGOs, and global forces to envision and invent better future.

Emerging Globalization Concerns

We discuss the development of globalization perspectives, contexts and the global interdependency loop in detail in our 2nd chapter on globalization. We familiarize the readers with rounds of globalization, globalization communication cycles, and process of globalization. We cannot ignore the iconoclasm of globalization, i.e. its challenge to tradition, a challenge to and overturning of traditional beliefs, customs, and values; the globalization convergence, i.e. the global adoption of social institutions and the process by which social institutions become adopted on a global scale; and the process by which a business or company becomes international or starts operating at an international level. We discuss about it in this chapter. Globalization does have two-way impact of geopolitics — the relationships that exist between a country's politics and its geography and population distribution and talents and skills quality of its people, and the influences that these will have on political and business relations among countries. This is a significant emerging concern. This geopolitics can set up our position in the globalization race.

As we stated earlier, globulation, glocalization and globalism are significant parameters for globalization and are significant for its operation, sustainability and impacts. We reiterate that glocalization, i.e. global plus local, is important parameter of globalization and its successes. The glocalization suggest adoption and influence of local cultural practices, local talents and also localizing the global trends. Globalism suggests a global culture of standardization of food, clothes, music, TV, films, and business styles. The divergent values and norms merge. Globulation is revolution from beyond. That is the global markets will force upon us the business practices and disciplines which we cannot generate internally.

This provides us background to search for, and deal with the Emerging Communication Practices and the Emerging Societies.

The three I's of interdependency loop, Interactions, and Information and information flow are essential for emerging communication practices in globulation, glocalization and globalism contexts.

Today, there is no weak or strong partner in the global interdependency loop. Anybody is a dominant player according to his strengths. India is a dominant player in computer software development because it can play on the strengths of its educated, talented and trained manpower in these areas. It is dominant in many areas of BPOs such as radiology, law and accountancy and KPOs in different areas because of its talent pool and expertise in these areas as compared to other countries. Comparatively, China is a dominant player where inexpensive, quality and good design manufacturing is concerned. Manufacturing could be in variety of garments and consumer goods, computer and other technology hardware, and cell phones, etc. It is developing technology hardware both off-shoring and indigenous. Its people have inherent expertise and knack for these areas. Whereas, it may not be good in running basic BPOs like call centers as it lacks pool of English speaking personnel. These and other developing countries are selling their ideas, products and services in their expertise areas may be to developed countries like USA, Middle Eastern rich countries and even the emerging countries. Thus they all seek to collaborate on one another's expertise. Collaboration is the business model for globalization.

To be in the global interdependency loop, one must have the requisite information and that is essential. But more significant is how it flows and to whom it flows; whether it is vertical, horizontal or circular among countries sharing interests on different fronts. Even it is equally significant if the information flow is vertical, horizontal or circular among different segments of a population in a country.

Interaction among people, different societies and among countries creates circular communications to bring convergence of ideas, products and services and mutual understanding among all the players in these contexts to deliver them according to the specific demands. We may talk about global culture but still every country has its own cultural practices, work ethics, and human interactions in diversified fields and dominated by these cultural practices. These are developed within the framework of globulation, glocalization and globalism contexts. These three contexts do govern how we communicate globally and emerging communication practices.

These three I's dominate various domains of people's lives such as politics, social and economic structures and functions, health, development, urbanization, rural development, business, digital divide, i.e. use and reach of communication channels. We learn, borrow and apply many practices to our culture specific situations and endeavor to find the best fit with our cultural practices vis-à-vis communication practices. The boundary of our cultural and global practices does overlap.

Interdependency loop in its wider connotation, when viewed positively is inter-reliance, inter-collaboration and inter-operability. But when looked at from negative point of view, this is real interdependency where it becomes survival issue bringing some negative post issues effects. USA is dependent on Middle-Eastern oil countries for oil, and these countries are dependent for petrol dollar earnings. Both of them get into real interdependency loop. As we have observed such dependency have been causing hostilities, wars, untold hardships and coercion to take each other to ransom to reduce prices or make more profits. Interestingly, both are affluent but not ready to reduce their demands and offer concessions. The line of thinking for USA is, 'why I should lower my standard of living by consuming less oil. I can afford to pay appropriately for my demands'. Whereas, the oil rich countries would reason, 'it is our precious asset, they (USA) are in urgent need, why should not we earn most and live a luxurious life, they can take it or leave it'. The International politics play its leading role here.

The interesting point is both of them do not own the 'whole'. No doubt, Middle-Eastern oil countries own oil wells; but where will they be without the foreign technology to identify the oil wells, to drill and dredge them, to pump out the oil and refine it through special laid out pipes and refineries — the total production process and over and above to maintain those facilities. The two are interdependent on each other and actually nobody is the stronger or weaker partner; but to reap the benefits of oil both have to cooperate and collaborate.

Other Emerging Concerns

The information and information flow is basic for communication practices. It is basics of communications that we want information and knowledge about people and issues, situations past and present and existing practices to communicate these concerns. The information flow as well sharing of knowledge about a specific new practice is imperative if we want to learn more about it, experiment it, and apply it to our situations to find the best fit. Therefore, information flow and knowledge sharing is essential to switch over to global practices.

We have information-gap when the information is biased and is not disseminated to all segments of the society. Information-gap also occurs when people cannot grasp information due to lack of education, understanding and skills. It does happen when people do not get opportunities to access information due to social barriers. Narula (2006a) argues that info-gap blocks further knowledge about good practices and creates development-gap, low global participation and less innovative societies. Info-gap through lack of opportunities to access technology create digital divide. The socio-economic gap between have and have-nots has been existing since time immemorial and has been one of the causes of lower development for these groups but still societies on the whole have been moving ahead and progressing. But as we observe, the digital-divide of a large segment of population of country puts spoke in globalization.

Communication is democratic when individuals at all levels including local and grass-roots levels are considered for right to information affecting them and people around them. Democracy of communications suggests creating connectivity through various communication channels for majority of the people. It also suggests that these channels and its content be equally accessible to them.

The scenario has changed now. Different countries, different businesses and even individuals can choose where, with whom and in what segment they want to do business and on what mutually beneficial terms. The interdependency of developed, developing and emerging markets is not for economic subjugation but for mutual economic benefits and prosperity. Your best talents, best skills are in demand and sought for whichever country you may belong to. The flow of funds globally, flow of talents and skills globally and flow of businesses globally can not only interconnect economy but boost economy worldwide.

Investments are done by government, public, private partnerships in two ways: investment in people, and investment in infrastructure to boost economy of any country.

Both kinds of investments need right kind of policies, political will, and flow of funds. What is more challenging is that such investments do help the common person and are not beneficial for elite segment of the society only. In this context, communicating with financial markets befitting a country's economy is important both from the point of opening its economy to foreign investments and joint ventures as well exporting and investing globally in different countries to boost the domestic economy.

In global economy and globalization contexts, investment in people is important. The focus is on creating more jobs and developing people's skills and talents to match the new jobs.

This will create prosperity for people, lower unemployment and will eradicate poverty to some extent.

Globalization forces continue to grow, bringing with them successes as well as discontents. Our interests are to assess the changing Communication Practices' impacts at global level on society, attitudinal and behavioral changes, capacity strengthening, leadership and decision-making both potential and in real time. We think of individual empowerment, and a country's empowerment through global empowerment and vice versa. Few anecdotes highlight these concerns in later chapters.

Our observation is that changing social, political, and business practices do empower people and governments. But technology is the main facilitator in how these are communicated around the world, how best practices are chosen among many; and how they get visibility. Secondly, technology practices itself are continuously being innovated, expanding, and create empowerment for people and governments in diverse domains.

Summary

Global issues and its solutions are the emerging concerns and many emerging communication practices are coming up to deal with these through mutual strengths. The global interdependency loop of people, societies, cultures and businesses are bound by the constant search for Best, Next and Emerging Communication Practices. The three I's of Interdependency loop, Interactions, and Information and information flow are essential for emerging communication practices in globulation, glocalization and globalism contexts. In such scenario what will empower people most will be the democracy of communications around the world. These emerging perspectives make people and countries think about global interdependency loop and being in that loop at one point of time or the other.

Since the practitioners' intended messages aim at positive outcomes; so they look for pragmatic communication practices which have positive and desired effects and intended outcomes; as well as being acceptable to the targeted audience. Some of these best practices are either totally or incrementally innovative, or borrowed, or adaptive according to the lessons learnt. A best communication practice is specific to domain, society and segment of society. It is time bound. What is today best may not be the best because of ongoing changes in these variables. So we look for rather next effective practice.

Impacts of communication practices in the particular domain are impacting society, attitudinal and behavioral changes, capacity building and strengthening, economic and political choices. These changing practices communicated in the right perspective would empower people, government, NGOs, and global forces to envision and invent better future.

Globulation, Glocalization and Globalism; Globalization Convergence and Geopolitics are significant parameters for globalization and are significant for its operation, sustainability and impacts.

Thinking Global

2

Globalization

Businesses are getting continually redefined, and reinventing new ways of doing business in the global market place is no longer an option —— it is utter necessity.

Anonymous

Globalization is not just phenomena, nor passing trend but an international system here to stay. It is the integration of technology, information and capital across national borders that are creating a single global market place and society. This new system is influencing the domestic policies, market forces, and international relations of virtually every country. One cannot understand the morning news; the investments market trends unless one is into the system. *Integration is the key to globalization.*

We have gone through three rounds of globalization from political, social and technology perspectives. The technology perspective with progress in technologies set up the globalization of politics, social, economics and business practices and skills.

Rounds of Globalization

1st round of globalization: 1800-1920. There was flow of capital, trade and labor across borders. This was facilitated by low transportation costs and invention of railroads, steam engines, airplanes, ships that moved people and goods across borders. This era of global finance capitalism was broken by World War I, Great Depression and Russian Revolution. This fractured the world both physically and ideologically.

2nd round lasted 1945-1989. This was cold war system — an international system in which few powers such as USA and Russia dominated the political and economic scenario. There were treaties and pacts among the countries but all dealt and executed behind the curtain — the so called Iron Curtain. Globalization was occurring but only among the two countries and their leaders. The individuals and small businesses were not participating. Fall of Berlin Wall in 1989 ended this era.

3rd round and the present globalization era 1990 onwards are different in many respects. Technology is the binding force. It is different in kind and degree. There is a degree of intensity with which the world is tied together in a single market-place. A greater number of population and countries are participating. The governments, people, companies are participating in economic, political, social, and technological activities.

Globalization system has replaced cold war geopolitics as the defining force in world affairs today. The symbol of cold war was a wall, which divided everyone. The symbol of globalization is World Wide Web which unites everyone. The defining document of the cold war system was *The Treaty*. The defining document of globalization system is *The Deal.* If the defining anxiety of the cold war system was annihilation by an enemy you know all too well in a world that was fixed and stable, *the defining anxiety in Globalization is fear of rapid change from an enemy you cannot touch, feel or see — a sense that your life can be changed at any moment by anonymous economic and technological changes.* During the cold war system we reached the hotline between the White House and the Kremlin. A symbol that we were all divided but the two super powers were in charge. In the era of (present) globalization, we reach for the Internet—a symbol that we are all connected but nobody is in-charge. In cold war the most frequently asked question was 'how big is your missile? In globalization the most frequently asked question is 'how fast is your Modem?' (Josef Joffe review of the book *The Lexus and the Olive Tree* by Friedman Thomas 1999 Farrar, Straus & Giroux, New York).

Communication Scenario and Globalization

Fifties experienced another form of globalization through the development models such as Dominant Paradigm, Interdependent Model, Dependency Model, and Basic Needs Models. Dominant paradigm presented globalization perspective by modernizing the world, connecting it by media exposure and literacy on one hand and industrialization and urbanization on the other hand. They advocated that there would be global modernizing effect by trickle down effects from the developed world to the developing countries.

Interdependent Model in 60s advocated a global perspective for development. Developed countries wanted to be the dominating power both in business and values through ideological domination and ideological aggression. Ideological domination is conveyed through commercial communication networks, transnational marketing corporations. The ideological aggression results when the transnational corporations penetrate the political sphere via their control over modern technology, education and by their own ideological and economic logic. Their agendas were that the worldwide hierarchy of power and values should organize developing countries.

This interdependent approach implied that developing countries must develop in the context of political and economic realities of the developed countries. The offshoot of this is the dependency model where developing countries are faced with the problem of underdevelopment due to dependency created by the imposition of economic and political realities of the developed countries.

Dominating powers control the mass media channels and its content, create consumerism bias, aggravate dependency that unleash frustration among the low earning level population and leads to collective aggressiveness as an escape valve.

The dependency theorists argue that communication serves the purpose of the publicizing transnational interests only. They emphasize the use of interpersonal channels since mass media channels are caught in the dependency relationships. Later, these perspectives facilitated development communication models of

80s onward decades in developing countries to do development in their national contexts.

In 80s, Basic Minimum Needs Model advocated by United Nations presented a global perspective on improving the quality of life for people globally by at least providing people with the five basic minimum needs of food, shelter, health, education and employment. *This started with a global perspective on eradication of absolute and relative poverty.*

Thus, *earlier globalization perspectives had mixed concerns—development, power and cultural ideology domination, control of communication channels and the information disseminated through them and commerce controls.* These concerns were more authoritarian in nature and moved in one-way direction—from developed to developing and poor countries. These had some elements of exploitation.

The current globalization perspectives have their roots in the early vision of 40s, and development communication models of 50s through 70s decades. The driving forces for globalization today are military and security, trade and commerce, technology, media, development and tourism.

(Excerpts from *Handbook of Communication Models, Perspectives, Strategies,* 2006).

Globalization communication cycles has followed three cycles. From 1800 onwards the transportation revolution through railways and roadways vehicles, steamships and in 1900 onwards the airplanes were bringing the different geographies closer. From World War I onwards the costs of these transportation modes have been falling and that had brought the different world geographies closer and that was Globalization 1.0, and it shrank the world from a large size to a medium size. The second globalization communications cycle lasted from 1980–2000 when the falling costs of telecom and Personal Computers (PC) shrank the distances among various geographies and the world became very small. The third globalization communications cycle 2000 onwards is being driven by three factors: high-speed data connectivity pipes between geographies; the proliferation of PCs in all those geographies; and the convergence of software that uses this infrastructure to create a genuine global work platform.

Globalization 2.0 was the era of mainframe computing which was vertical — command and control oriented with companies and individuals organized in vertical silos. Globalization 3.0 is convergence of the global forces and combination of PC, microprocessor, Internet, fiber optics. These fostered and demanded new business practices of less command and control but more about connecting and collaborating horizontally. Collaborating horizontally and managing horizontally needed different set of skills.

Globalization process creates connectivity and convergence. It is understood from four contexts. One is cultural convergence. Second is political context, which is concerned about free flow of information. Third is economic context focusing on capitalism, consumerism, transnationalism, and globalization of western economic values. Fourth is media context focusing on media contribution to all the above-mentioned three contexts.

Global communication is imperative these days to connect to people globally not only on just one basis but across many countries because of growing needs and demands on many fronts, viz. political, economic, socio-cultural, technology, etc. A network of communication across countries, inter-country and cross-country leads to globalization. An interesting example is holding summits. *Globalization follows a circular model of communication.*

The communication revolution via cable TV, video, Internet and telecommunication, has brought the consumers in direct contact with evolving tastes all over the world.

Globalization gets growing into *cultural convergence* manifested in hardware and software transnational media products (telecommunication, video, TV), other commodities, business, banks, and advertising agencies, etc. Others think of cultural convergence as evident in things people think about, the ways in which they think, and which things are expressed through everyday social practices. Other aspect of 'cultural hybridize' arises from play of global forces through immigration, in search of employment opportunities and global trade.

Dominant Paradigm of development in 50s advocated that effects of modernization and industrialization would trickle down from developed to developing countries and from elite to the masses. Globalization model is different. It rather interconnects the parts. The frequent inter-country and cross-country interactions depend on their (each country's) needs and demand to interact. The force of globalization shifts power away from governments to private capital in whatever market it takes place.

The forces of interdependence of nation do create a close knit global economy. Transnational Communication (TNC) is the primary agent of globalization through media and multi-corporate. The driving force is revolutions in Information Communication Technologies (ICTs). TNC with interlinked interests in commodities, manufacturing, banking, finance, and its hold on technology can change international systems and can create a transnational world order – where national sovereignty will give way to TNC interests. Globalization and transnational cultural process is for their 'iconoclasm'; that is their power in forcing us to rethink critical frameworks.

Iconoclasm of globalization refers to rapidly developing process of complex interconnection among the societies, cultures, institutions, and individuals worldwide. It is a process which involves compression of time and space, shrinking distances through a dramatic reduction in time either physical or representational – to cross them, so making the world seem smaller and bringing human beings closer to one another. It is also a process that stretches social relationships from local contexts to global contexts.

The iconoclastic implications of the concept of globalization are that it challenges the familiar ways of describing the world. It threatens to destroy the images of the world cherished in so many intellectual and critical traditions, displacing or forcing reexamination of certain givens of social and cultural analysis.

The iconoclasm of globalization lies in the implicit demand to re-envisage the world that arises once the nature of the complex global interconnectedness and the process of time-space compression and action at distance are recognized. Re-envisioning is disturbing and inevitably involves the destruction of shibboleths, many of which may be linked to political and moral commitments. But re-envisioning is not the same as revisionism.

The globalization is not static like cold war but dynamic on-going process. It involves integration of markets, nation-states and technologies to a degree never witnessed before enabling individuals, corporations, nation-states to reach the world farther, faster and deeper and cheaper than ever before.

Global has two meanings. One is the traditional definition of international, which has messages, data, or people going across or through some kind of barriers, boundaries or constraints, whether it be the encoding or decoding process from one human being to other, or the artificial borders between nation-states. The other definition concerns issues that are common enough to group of people to transcend traditional boundaries.

The driving idea behind globalization is free-market capitalism. The more you let the market force rule and open your economy to free trade and competition, the more efficient and flourishing your economy will be.

Globalization has its own defining technologies—computerization, miniaturization, digitization, satellites, fiber-optics, and the Internet. These technologies help in defining the globalization perspective of integration. Once the country accepts this perspective, its elites leap into the system and try to locate themselves in global context.

Globalization has its own demographic pattern – a rapid acceleration of the movement of people from rural areas and agriculture to urban areas and urban lifestyles, more intimately linked with global food, fashions, markets and entertainment trends.

Globalization is built around three balances which might affect and overlap one another. First is the traditional balance between nation-state. The second balance is between nation-states and global markets. The third balance is between the individuals and the nation-states. Because globalization has brought down many walls that limited the movements and reach of the people, it has simultaneously wired the world into networks. It has given more power to individuals to influence both markets and nation-states. Now we have super empowered individuals. All of these super empowered individuals can act on the world stage without the traditional mediation of governments, corporations, or any other public or private institutions. *To understand globalization is to understand the complex interaction between all these three actors.*

The only way to understand globalization is to arbitrage all the six dimensions of politics, culture, national security, balance of power, financial markets and technology. Different weights have to be assigned to different perspectives at different times in different situations. *But it is always the interaction of all of them together that really defines international relations today.*

Global integration of technology, finance, trade and information in a way is influencing the wages, interest rates, jobs opportunities, the living standards, wars and weather patterns all over the world. Thus, globalization is a system that is influencing all these factors and trends.

Globalization Convergence

Four types of convergence occur to create globalization. These convergences focus on connectivity for globalization. First, is the convergence with the new fields with new processes for modernization and development. Second, convergence is the development of business personnel infrastructure to deal with globalization and development of new set of business practices and skills. Third, convergence is giving access to billions of people from many developing countries to converge with the new fields with new processes. Fourth, convergence is in the contexts of political, cultural, social, economic and media practices.

First convergence is with the new fields with new processes for modernization and development by media exposure and literacy on one hand and industrialization and urbanization on the other hand.

Second convergence occurred (though the global forces may be there) with the emergence of large cadre of managers, innovators, business consultants, business schools, designers, IT specialists, CEO, and workers to get comfortable with the new system, develop the horizontal collaboration and value creation processes and habits that could take advantage of this new playing field. In short, *the convergence of these global forces beget the convergence of new set of business practices and skills, and then these two begin to mutually reinforce each other.* The new ways of doing things make the information technologies more valuable; and new and better information technologies make possible the new ways of doing things.

Third convergence gave access to people from so many countries in China, India, Eastern Europe, Latin America, Russia and Central Asia (in collaborating horizontally) in 90s to join the free-market game when their economic and political systems opened up. Billions of people converged with the new fields with new processes. There was triple convergence of new players, new playing field and developing new process and habits for horizontal collaboration. The scale of global community that is able to participate in all sorts of discovery and innovations was never seen before. The winners will be those who learn the habits, processes and skills most quickly and able to compete with others efficiently and they could be from any country. Nobody will rule anybody anymore. It is about how you can create opportunity for yourself, hold on to that, keep creating new opportunities and thrive. The rule is about efficiency, competition and collaboration and about being a player. The triple convergence is not only going to affect how people prepare themselves for work, and how countries organize their economies and geopolitics. Overtime, it is going to reshape their political identities, how communities and companies redefine themselves, how individuals balance their different identities as consumers, employees, shareholders, stakeholders and citizens and the role of government gets redefined. The image of countries and its people has to be recalibrated.

Fourth convergence focuses on cultural resources and practices, political context, which is concerned about free flow of information, economic context focusing on capitalism, consumerism, transnationalism, and globalization of western economic values, and the media context focusing on media contribution to all the above-mentioned contexts.

Forces that Created the Globalization

Workflow software: The self-organizing communities. There are two basic forms of open-sourcing — the intellectual commons movement and the free software movement. Intellectual commons form of open-sourcing has its roots in the self-organized collaborative communities of academics and scientists who come together through private networks and now through Internet to pool their brainpower and share insights around a particular academic or science issue. Open source is peer reviewed science to make science and innovations, to increase the knowledge in the world and sometimes to build business out of it. Second is development of free open-source software for computer such as Linux operating system as differentiated from commercial software of Microsoft. Free software movement remains inspired by the ethical ideal that software should be free and available to all and the observations that it can bridge the digital divide.

Outsourcing and offshoring: Both of these factors are interlinked to the economies of the developed world. There is interconnecting of markets and knowledge. Such globalization has its challenges though no doubt creating global prosperity and economic growth for themselves.

In-sourcing: Synchronizing global supply chains large and small by delivering packages (UPS, courier services, air cargo). Secondly, UPS handling and repairing (the Toshiba laptop, HCL printer in their repair shops).

In-forming by web search through search engines Yahoo, Google, Microsoft. These do not push their products and services on their customers but build collaborative systems that enable customers to pull on their own and then respond to what they pull.

Internet adds to information, knowledge and instant messages and connectivity. It provides forum, enables consumers to gather around a topic that are meaningful to them in ways that are impractical and impossible offline. The in-forming makes the world transparent.

Digital, mobile, personal and virtual further empowers all forms of collaborations. There is triple convergence. When the workflow software and hardware converge in, then a single machine can offer scanning, e-mailing, printing and faxing and copying. A single mobile phone offers phone, e-mailing, picture-taking, and video-conferencing and may be many more features to come.

Global supply chains: The convergence of technology and events allowed India, China and many other countries to become part of the global supply chain for services and manufacturing, creating explosion of wealth among the middle classes of the two biggest nations and giving them huge stake in the success of globalization. The world had gotten too small, too fast for human beings and their political systems to adjust to it in a stable manner. Globalization success and discontents mean differently to countries, companies, communities and individuals.

Globalization Challenges

Globalization poses challenges but it offers tremendous opportunities. If you want to be out of the globalization system, and then accept the fact that you will have less access to capital, technology and ultimately a lower standard of living for your people. The biggest challenge is how to give citizens a sense that they can exercise their will not only over their own government but also on some of the global forces shaping their lives.

There are tensions between the globalization system and the ancient forces of culture, geo, tradition and community. The traditional boundaries between culture, politics, technology, finance, national security and ecology are disappearing. You cannot explain one without referring to the others. You have to arbitrage information from one to other perspective and weave together an integrated perspective of the world perspective.

Backlashes of the system are other challenges

The spread of free markets and democracy around the world permits people to globalize but it also presents both positive and negative challenges. On the positive side, there is challenge of democratizing technology, information and capital in globalization. On the negative side, terrorism is globalized since it knows no national borders. It is a big challenge to counteract this.

Politics, culture and security shape the financial markets. But the major dimension of technology from Internet to satellite telecommunications shapes the globalization of financial markets. The rise and fall of financial markets depended on how nations and individuals interacted with one another. The advances in technology are greater facilitator in this respect.

Significant Factors for Globalization

Four factors are significant for globalization to occur and to let it sustain and have impact on nation-states, businesses, companies and individuals. These are: democratization of technology, democratization of finance, democratization of information, democratization of decision-making and information flow. The building blocks of democratization are transparency and standards. The push for common global standards is going to be intensified since Internet defines commerce, freedom of the press and non-corruption. This kind of democratization will give flexibility, legitimacy and sustainability.

Democratization of technology is enabling more and more people with home computers, cable system, cellular phones and Internet connections to reach farther and farther into more countries, faster and faster, deeper and deeper and cheaper and cheaper than ever before in the history. It has enabled millions of people around the world to get connected and exchange information.

The democratization of technology is the result of several innovations in 80s. Advance technology in telecommunication has brought down the cost of telephone call. Computerization, miniaturization, digitization, advancement in compression technology and microchip technology has resulted in higher and faster computing power. All these innovations have reinforced, and been reinforced by the revolution in digitization.

Digitization has turned voices, sounds, movies, TV signals, music, color pictures, words, documents, numbers, computing language, and any other form of data into computer bits and then transfers them by telephone lines, fiber-optics and satellites around the world. Computing bits are 1's and 0's and digitization reduces these 1's and 0's into different codes; which are transmitted through telecommunications and decodes and reconstituted into something very close to the original. *The process of digitization is central to understand the globalization era.*

Democratization of finance helped us how we invest globally in 80s. This was enhanced by the international system of fixed exchange rates, strict controls on international flows of capital. Developed countries gradually democratized capital markets opening them to any foreign traders who wanted to play and then developing countries have been following suit; opening their markets for foreign investments, as well foreign investors are finding these emerging markets lucrative for investments and returns. These factors together are creating economic growth and healthy economies.

Democratization of information is how we look at the world. Satellites, cellular technology, Internet and cable TV make us see through any conceivable wall. More people are able to tell their stories through these means. People's aspiration and motivations go higher to match the others around when they see them, hear them. They do not want to be left behind. It is an environment where we increasingly know how others are living. Globalization of information is constantly letting people know how others live and that gives impetus to their aspirations, and achievements. It is important that economic development within countries create larger and new middle classes around the world with their natural demand for participation in decision making and political pluralism.

Democratization of decision-making and information flow: Microchip immune deficiency happens when governments, companies, fail to inoculate themselves against the changes of globalization. They are resistant to increased productivity, wages, living standards, knowledge use and competitiveness and become too slow to respond to the challenges of the fast world. In this model, a few people at the top are the decision-makers; all at the middle and bottom carry the decisions. This happens in centrally planned, centrally controlled and top-down directed governments and societies. *But for globalization, one follows the model of decentralization and people's participation. There is command and connect and not control and command.* There is both vertical and horizontal communication among people and leaders, among people and people.

These four factors have changed how we communicate, how we see the world and how we invest. It is not whether we globalize that matters but how we globalize is important and significant.

Within the globalization framework, the two other factors of *Globulation* and *Glocalization* are significant for its operation, sustainability and impacts. Globulation is revolution from beyond. That is the global markets will force upon us the business practices and disciplines which we cannot generate internally. Glocalization is localizing the global trends.

Globalism: Globalism discourse is based on three levels: values, knowledge and interests. The focus is on global understanding and global consciousness. It is awareness that local events have global consequences and understanding of global impact.

Globalism suggests a global culture of standardization of food, clothes, music, TV, films, business styles. The divergent values and norms merge. It is not true that these processes lead to global integration. The same processes propelling globalization can integrate as well as disintegrate it. Disintegration occurs when value system that dominates globalization is refused. In a way this also protects weaker units. Interdependence does not merge nations into larger units. Global transactions can create more cooperation, competition as well as conflicts.

Eight habits of highly effective countries

Friedman (2000) suggests that eight habits of highly effective countries can help their populations participate in globalization successfully and effectively people: i) How wired is your country by Internet, telecommunications and other technologies. ii) How fast is your country in picking new global trends and practices? iii) How much does your country weigh, i.e. the substitution effect whereby knowledge and information technologies are increasingly substituted by creation of products in economic value. iv) Does your country dare to be open. Keeping your economy as open as possible will give multiple benefits in globalization system. Knowledge is the key to economic growth in this era and if you close your economy to best brains in the world or best technology in the world you are liable to fall behind fast. v) How good is your country at making friends? In a global economy you cannot survive in certain industries unless you compete on a global basis and for that you need alliances. The sheer amount of scientific and technical knowledge needed to develop certain complex products need the pooled resources of several companies. The only way these companies can recover their costs for research and development is by selling worldwide and not just in their small domestic market. This also needs alliances. Thus for economic security you need alliances in international economic realm. We need more partners and alliances for the national security also and for countering the terrorism which crosses all borders. These transnational issues can be more threatening.

Further, vi) How good is your country in managing globalization. Management and leadership matter to attract other countries to be interested in investing in your resources and businesses and doing business with you. The other countries would be assessing how your management and leadership, both political and business understand the four democratizations and know how to take advantage of them. Can they synthesize six different dimensions of politics, technology, finance, culture, national security and ecology at the same time and can they do information arbitrage. vii) How good is your country's brand? In today's globalized world it is important that the powerful country and powerful company need to have 'strong brand' as well as strong brand image for product and services to attract consumers and investors. When both of these are satisfied, they associate with the brand and country and are willing to pay even a premium price. To build brand equity, the company needs to distinguish its products and services from others in the market and align with marketing and advertising to deliver what it says about products. viii) As more and more people start to realize that their country can go for prosperity and they see through exposure to technology how people live in style and prosperity. They are going to ask why their government has not chosen policies for prosperity. People's demands and willingness to participate in implementation of such policies can push them for global products and services.

In today's globalization system, it does not matter where you are and who you are but what you are that matters the most and on that depends the choices you make for prosperity in this system.

Globalization and geopolitics: It does not end geopolitics. But it does constrain them to indulge in wars. Today's globalization version is – economic integration, digital integration, ever-widening connectivity of individuals and nations, spreading capitalist values and networks to the remotest corners of the world and growing dependence on golden strait-jacket and electronic herd. Whosoever is plugged to this system would refrain from war for its economic security. *It increases the incentive for not going to war as it increases the cost of wars in losing economic security in the international realm.*

But globalization influences geopolitics in many other ways. They create new sources of pressures on the countries to change how they organize themselves. This would come from the businesses, investments and consumer goods and services and from super-empowered individuals and not from pressures of military incursions of one country to another. *This is invisible invasion of information and private capital.*

But there are more civil wars between the pro-globalization and anti-globalization; between globalist in each society and localist in each society; between those who benefit from it and those suffer or are left behind.

As Friedman (2000) suggests, *the only way to be effective in globalization system is always moving back and forth among the economic, national security, political, cultural, environmental and technological dimensions and assigning different weights to each in different contexts.*

Glocalization

Cultural Practices and Filters

People are concerned about the *cultural homogenization* because of globalization. It is argued that world is much richer if the colorations and diversities are sustained and encouraged with different cultures. You lose your bearings when your culture is uprooted; 'there are two ways to make you feel homeless. One way is to destroy your home and other way is to make your home look like and feel like everybody's home'.

Cultural practices will change to certain extent when new products and services whether food, clothing, values and behavior are exposed to people from across the world through media and personal influence. They are liable to influence them. The only hope is that people will develop multiple filters to prevent their culture from being erased by homogenization pull and push of global capitalism. Cultures that are not robust enough are likely to be wiped away with the speed and force of globalization.

The most important filter is the ability to glocalize. Healthy glocalization is the ability of a culture, when it is encountered by cultural influences of a strong culture, to absorb influences that naturally fit into their cultural practices to enrich them and to resist those which are totally alien and misfit to their cultural values. They compartmentalize those which are different but can nevertheless be enjoyed as different from their culture.

Glocalization should aim to assimilate aspects of globalization into your country and culture in a way that adds to your growth and diversity without overwhelming you.

Glocalism is trial and error process but is a necessary one. Globalization is less threatening to those cultures which can glocalize. Some cultures, while glocalizing in a healthy way may lose their identity subtly and slowly.

The other filter is that local talent is hired, has a job with the growing economy and globalization is not taking that away. This created the 'livability issue'. The filters of new middle classes, the cultural and environmental filters are created. All filters have to work together to have any impact.

When cultures are homogenized they also lose social cohesion. Culture at its best can be powerful forms of voluntary restraint in human behavior. It can give life structure and meaning. It sanctions a whole lot of habits, behavioral restraints, expectations, and traditions that pattern life and hold societies together at their core. *When unrestrained globalization destroys the cultures and environments, it destroys the necessary underlying fabric of communal life.*

Emerging Societies

Emerging societies along with emerging markets is necessary for sustainable globalization. You cannot build emerging societies if you are destroying the cultural foundations that cement the society and give it self-confidence and cohesion to interact with the world. We need sustainable community depending on sustainable culture and environment for sustainable globalization. Globalization will be sustainable depending upon how well each of us manages the filters to protect our culture and environment. It should be an efficient exchange of cultures creating unity in diversity.

There is growing awareness among leaders of the world that both *emerging market* as well an *emerging society* are necessary to succeed in globalization system. It does not pay to privatize your economy in a societal and governance vacuum. It is critically important both for the investors and politicians to broaden their definition of what constitutes a healthy emerging market by looking at what constitutes a healthy emerging society. Putting the market before the society is creating trouble and disappointment. Emerging society is graded on the quality of their governing software, their judicial system, procedures for settling disputes, social safety net, rule of law and operating economic systems.

In *The Winners-Take-All-Society* Frank and Cook advocate that globalization has played important role in the expansion of inequality. They note that a global market is created by reducing or eliminating trade barriers and tariffs, by slashing travel costs, internal markets being deregulated, information being freely and cheaply disseminated across borders. You put all these factors together; you end up with a situation in which the potential market for any goods or services, for any doctor, writer, lawyer, athlete or academic extends from one end of the world to the other. This unprecedented openness and opportunity for mobility encourages companies, industries and professionals to cover this worldwide market as well as to face the competition from worldwide. Whosoever emerges winner in the particular field, can be potential winner in any country worldwide and win acclaim and royalties from everywhere at once. They comment that in this global village, the top player can deliver the best product and earn enormous profits.

Frank and Cook point that gap between the winners and those with less and poorly skills will widen. When winners take all markets, the inequalities expand within countries and between countries. These inequalities are becoming the most disturbing social products of this system.

It becomes politically destabilizing when cultural backlash is combined with economically aggrieved by globalization backlash. Then cultural, economic, and political backlashes are interwoven for political movements to seek power.

Globalization Stress

We learn to strike the balance between the globalization's inherently empowering and humanizing power to its inherently disempowering and dehumanizing power. Politics of sustainable globalization needs more than a correct picture of what is happening in the world. It needs right balance of policies and social safety nets.

Even if we can get at the right politics, geopolitics and geo-economics for sustainable globalization; we do need set of policies to protect and preserve the particular culture. Globalization and Internet may connect people who have never known each other before but it cannot create the intimacy and cohesion of a community created by face to face relationships within the same culture, following the same cultural practices. *Balancing globalization and own cultural practices is something every society has to work everyday. A healthy society is one that can emulate that model.*

At its best and worst, it is mainly globalization of American culture and cultural icons. America has the global arrogance (of which America is blamed —there is no balance, no counterpoise whatever you say is law.) when its culture and economic clout are so powerful and widely diffused that they know they do not need to occupy other people to influence their lives. But it is different from American imperialism where there is extension of power or authority, influence over others in the interest of political, economic, cultural domination of America over other countries.

The combination of Americanization and globalization has made it powerful. It may bother many countries that America sends its culture, values, economics, technologies, and lifestyles everywhere whether others want them or not. Another popular reaction to it is that they complain about America bitterly throwing weight around and at the same time they sit back and enjoy American driven technologies and power.

The above scenario is changing to some extent when America is realizing the importance of emerging markets of India contributing to their cultural icons by software technologies, business and management models and values, quality pharmaceutical researches. China contributing to life style changes through consumer goods as well the other oil countries facilitating their economy.

There are angry men and women who are anti-globalization for various reasons such as the economic, political backlash and the cultural invasion that gets into their homes, family, and community life. These super-powered angry men and women can be angry and less violent such as computer hackers; they are little angrier and little more violent such as LTTE who put Sri Lanka Government's electronic system out of gear in 1997 by overwhelming it with e-mails. Then there are really angry and more violent who would bomb the facilities and kill people on the go. They express their rage against globalization by rejecting its tenets and at the same time using the global technology of Internet to bombs.

Other ways in which they reject globalization is that it is just too connected, too intrusive, too unfair for too many people, and too dehumanizing.

Summary

It is the integration of technology, information and capital across national borders that is creating a single global market place and society. This new system is influencing the domestic policies, market forces, and international relations of virtually every country. We have gone through three rounds of globalization from political, social and technology perspectives from 1800 to 2000. Globalization communication has followed three cycles during these decades. Globalization process creates connectivity and convergence is imperative. Four types of convergence occur to create the process of globalization.

Globalization follows a circular model of communication and creates the iconoclasm of globalization that refers to rapidly developing process of complex interconnection among the societies, cultures, institutions, and individuals worldwide.

It challenges the familiar and traditional ways of describing the world, and displacing or forcing reexamination of certain givens of social and cultural analysis.

Forces that created the globalization are outsourcing, offshoring, in-sourcing, in-informing, and global supply chains. Globalization poses challenges but it offers tremendous opportunities. The spread of free markets and democracy around the world permits people to globalize but it also presents both positive and negative challenges.

Four factors are significant for globalization to occur and to let it sustain and have impact on nation-states, businesses, companies and individuals. These are: democratization of technology, democratization of finance, democratization of information and information flow, and democratization of decision-making. These four factors have changed how we communicate, how we see the world and how we invest. It is not whether we globalize that matters but how we globalize is important and significant.

Globulation, glocalization and globalism are other significant factors for its operation, sustainability and impacts.

Globulation is revolution from beyond. That is the global markets will force upon us the business practices and disciplines which we cannot generate internally. Glocalization is localizing the global trends. Globalism suggests a global culture of standardization of food, clothes, music, TV, films, business styles. The divergent values and norms merge.

We need more partners and alliances for business, national security also and for countering the terrorism which crosses all borders. These transnational issues can be more threatening. People's demands and willingness to participate in implementation of such policies can push them for global products and services.

Globalization does influence geopolitics in many other ways. They create new sources of pressures on the countries to change how they organize themselves. This would come from the businesses, investments and consumer goods and services and super-empowered individuals and not from pressures of military incursions of one country to another.

There is growing awareness among leaders of the world that both *emerging market* as well an *emerging society* are necessary for sustainable globalization. Sustainable globalization needs right balance of policies and social safety nets.

In today's globalization system, it does not matter where you are, and who you are, but what matters the most is what you are, and on that depends the choices you make for prosperity in this system.

Communication Technologies: Bridges

3

Facilitator or Divider

There is technology gap between You and New
There is technology gap between have and have-nots
The Technology Bridges facilitate.

Anonymous

Democracy of Communications

Communication is democratic when individuals at all levels including local and grassroots levels are considered for right to information affecting them and people around them. When individual is an active subject of communication and not just the inept object. This suggests that individual is actively involved in communication process and various messages are exchanged democratically for convergence and mutual understanding. For example, if we handle the problem of poverty we want to hear their (poor people's) voices and concerns. If we want economy to prosper we need to listen to the views, and understand the perspectives of the high-end, middle-end and the low-end consumers to the businesses, to the policy makers, to governance, and even what the global demands and perspective are. Politically, if we want a stable government, we cannot ignore the interests of the citizens and civil society. There have to be public discourses and dialogues to understand their dynamics and demands, and understanding of political will as well its limitations. This is democratization of communication. Earlier, even in 80s McBride has advocated democracy of information exchange between the developed and developing countries to understand international perspectives democratically without any bias. This was the start of new world information order (NWICO) in 80s. Though the advent of active global initiatives in all walks of life since 90s has led to more information exchange globally and of high order and about higher concerns.

Further, democracy of communications suggests creating connectivity through various communication channels for majority of the people. It also suggests that these channels and their contents be equally accessible to them. But that is neither pragmatic nor the realty and perhaps not politically correct and desirable. Though such stance is significant and imperative for being effective in any sphere of life.

Ideally, we do not expect censorship and scrambling of various communication channels when we feel we have right to know and be informed. Communication channels such as Internet, TV, radio, telecommunication, films have all crossed the national borders, have wider reach, and are globally accessible, viewable and have impact on people's personal and professional lives, businesses, and economy of their country.

Therefore, it is not feasible for countries to talk about censorship of accessibility of communication channels and its contents; rather they can regulate them by national and international regulations for healthy growth, for utilizing benefits, and have positive impact on lifestyles, businesses and overall growth of economy and material and social prosperity vis-à-vis development.

This does empower people. Such communication strategies, policies and healthy attitude of governance, business and people empower people in global contexts. *We are experiencing and witnessing such change in communication practices – no censorship but regulations to create healthy growth of communication channels both nationally and internationally.*

We expect no censorship but regulations for communication channels and its contents would empower people. But it is equally important that majority of the people should have physical and social access to both media and interpersonal communication channels. This will be real empowerment of people. Physical access is the purchasing power and closer contact point where community access is provided and equally important is the social access where people are barred communication due to caste, creed, class, ethnic and gender differentiations.

We mentioned in the earlier chapter 'thinking global' that four factors are significant for globalization to occur and to let it sustain and have impact on nation-states, businesses, companies and individuals. In this chapter we focus on how the two factors of democracy of information and information flow, technology factor — new and old technologies and innovations in technologies are creating connectivity and information flow, awareness and knowledge about global issues facilitating global empowerment. We discuss and raise the points whether technology is divider or facilitator for global empowerment.

Democracy of Information and Information Flow

Information about any subject matter, geo-area, culture, or nation is basic for creating any kind of awareness and knowledge about them. Both, creating information and disseminating and diffusing information to create awareness and knowledge are equally important. More important is sifting the relevant information for people from the overload of information. Relevant information makes its effective. All these three suggest information flow and sharing of information. *Information is power and acquiring the relevant information empowers you to deal with the issues effectively.*

In national contexts, the information flow on issues and sub-issues creates awareness about them and stimulate knowledge for acceptance and rejection or implementation of the issues through public discourses and dialogues. In global contexts, awareness and knowledge through information flow creates globalization impact on people's lifestyles, businesses and economy and overall cultural identity of the nation.

Information flow is a continuous process — discarding some information and adding more; disseminating where and to whom it is relevant. The democracy of information flow suggests that disseminating information to where and to whom it is relevant should be the guideline. It also leads to transparency and accountability. It is valuable when the opinion leaders at the village level create and disseminate information to lowly educated and low-connected villagers in India about specific development programs. It facilitates implementation of such programs. But it can be disastrous when such leaders would intentionally withhold information, misinterpret or mis-communicate and filter it to suit their personal biases for certain segment of society or for the program itself. Here both the opinion leadership communication channel and programs will fail.

Democracy of information affects nations and societies in two ways: on one hand affecting lives, values, needs and demands of different layers of society and on the other hand, affecting the businesses and the economy of the country. The second has also overall effect on the people's lives. Further, democracy of information creates and sustains national businesses and economy in globalization contexts.

Here is an interesting scenario. In India in 2005 Government grants citizens' right to know. Have you ever been told by a government officer that your passport application, or even the power connection to your house will not be processed unless palms are greased? There is now a way to fight back. With the Right to Information Act of 2005, passed by Parliament, finally coming into effect across the country, any one can demand answers from the government by approaching each department.

This new law that comes into effect guarantees every Indian the right to know exactly what the government is up to. All this information will be accessible simply by filling up a form. Will this work?

So far nine states including Delhi, Karnataka and Jammu & Kashmir had enacted their own state laws on right to information, which allows citizens to ask for just about any government project or even the status of their passport or the laying of power and water connections. For this, each State and the Centre appoint information commissioners.

Public rights activists say that this is one of the most important legislations since independence, which will not only make the government more accountable but will give the citizens a greater say in the governance. However, campaigners also say their next challenge will be to ensure that people get this right.

The idea of applying to a government office to get the desired information for a small fee (certainly not a bribe) is a powerful one to finally have something that will make the unyielding officialdom accountable to everyone.

And, if an official denies you information, not only does he have to give an explanation, but if proven wrong, he will have to pay a fine at the rate of Rs. 250 per day for the number of days he made you run around. It is certainly a powerful idea for a democracy where official apathy is synonymous with governance.

The central RTI Act gives structure to this idea. There will be a structure of state and central information commissioners with quasi-judicial powers to oversee the implementation of the law. Every district in the country will have to appoint a public information officer ready to relay information to applicants. Every government department and even institutions which are supported by the government — no matter what is the degree of support — are open to scrutiny under the law.

To make RTI Act more citizen friendly and delivering information, a nationwide awareness-cum-assistance campaign has been launched in India where people will be encouraged not to pay bribes. The 'Drive against Bribes' campaign began on July 1, 06 and will be on till July 15, 06. Nearly 1500 trained volunteers are available at centers in 48 cities around the country. Eight media partners and more than 700 civil society groups are a part of this initiative. Volunteers are even educating villagers on using RTI. Over 11,60,000 Indians have pledged never to pay a bribe again as the national anti-bribery campaign enters its eighth day. Thousands more have successfully used the RTI or the Right to Information Law. Common citizens are using the Right to Information as a powerful tool in order to hold governments accountable. People have used it in various ways ranging from addressing issues related to their daily interface with government authorities to influencing major government policies.

Here is another story: Uday returned to the capital from Germany where he had been working for several years. The first thing that literally hit him on his arrival in the city, were the potholes on the road to his home in Vasant Kunj residential colony in South Delhi.

When no repairs were carried out on the road, which had been laid recently, Uday filed a questionnaire under the Delhi Right to Information Act, asking the Municipal Corporation of Delhi to explain why the road was in such a bad condition. Uday also asked for the road to be inspected in his presence.

"It was a miracle. One week before the inspection the road was being built and even the pothole, which had come up the night before was perfectly filled the next morning," said Uday.

We, in India did not make much progress in globalization of businesses till 90s. The economic reforms of 90s onwards created better ambiance for globalization. More important was the better information flow. Till 90s the information flow about business information, government rules, economy, etc. were not accessible, transparent, accountable to foreign business parties from home and abroad due to bureaucratic snags and inefficient and lackadaisical attitudes and that did discourage doing business in India to a certain extent.

We suggest the changing communication practices of giving right to information to its citizens and information flow for people and businesses at home and abroad makes issues transparent, accountable and participatory for finding solutions and dealing with them. We do expect that such information flow may not bypass the lowly that needs it most perhaps.

Communication Technology as Facilitator

The focus is on democratizing technology in its facilitator's role. The technology dynamics highlight the new information communication technologies, its channels and the functionality of the conventional and new ICTs in people's lives. Global community recognizes that ICTs can play a major role in social and economic development and contribute significantly towards poverty eradication. The efforts are to improve people's lives by building partnerships and information systems that provide access to knowledge for development.

The key development parameters of the recent past are not predominantly about economic productivity, but have more to do with equity and access to information and enhancing the knowledge base. Thus the most important assets of nations are not raw materials, physical goods or economic production, but human resources keyed into the information and knowledge revolution (Schoolnet Research, 2002). There has to be analytical syntheses of how the regions deal with issues and concerns that come to the fore as new technologies are deployed to advance the socioeconomic development.

Series of discussions go on about challenges related to ICTs, i) bridging the digital divide, ii) Internet governance, iii) the social, political and cultural aspects of ICT, iv) appropriate ICTs, and v) how ICTs for development contributes to the building of information societies in the regions. The government, industry and civil society face a major challenge in terms of converging divergent interests.

While other regions of the world, such as Europe and the America, shift progressively towards regional integration, the Asia-Pacific region faces the threat of fragmentation. This challenge is so important that it will continue to be present in the dynamics of development well beyond the Tunis phase of the World Summit on the Information Society (WSIS). The WSIS forum addressed "Information Technology and Collaborative Development", focusing on the practical issues of ICT strategy and policy for effective development (2006).

Friedman (2005) argues that fragmentation may constitute a very important risk in the current globalization process, which helps to "flatten" the world. The globalization process involves workflow software adoption, open-sourcing, outsourcing, off-shoring, supply-chaining, in-sourcing and other components. While some talk about the knowledge society or the information economy, others like Friedman, argue using the metaphor of the "Flat World". They posit that, while some rituals and debates are taking place at WSIS and elsewhere, globalization forces to continue to grow (bringing with them successes as well as discontent) and that some economies may face a new type of dependency within our networked society which may be manifested in very different ways from those anticipated.

If appropriation of information and ICTs are the building blocks of an information economy and of a knowledge society, there are four major and urgent challenges confronting us: i) There are stifling copyright restrictions and intellectual property mechanisms asserted by economies with well-developed ICT industries. This stranglehold on knowledge restricts access to technologies as the main cause of the digital divide. ii) The issue regarding the urgency of including and involving all sectors of society in ICT policy dialogues. In Asia, where governments and inter-governmental organizations tend to dominate the policy-making arena, we should ensure that ICT policy dialogues include all sectors particularly civil society, which is often the missing player in these discussions. iii) We need a participatory development communication paradigm that goes beyond the modernization and dependency paradigms. iv) The challenge of role of human capital in building the knowledge economy, and its central function of nurturing information societies.

World Summit on the Information Society—16 to 18 November, 2005 held in Tunis and earlier summit in Geneva in 2003 focused on issues in ICT global policies.

The World Summit on the Information Society (WSIS) in Tunis — the second phase, poses more questions than solid agreements, in spite of the official promise to turn it into a "summit of solutions".

The number of countries seeking to control the Internet has risen rapidly in the recent years. Mustering powerful and at times compelling arguments — "securing intellectual property rights," "protecting national security," "preserving cultural norms and religious values," and "shielding children from pornography and exploitation" — extensive filtering and surveillance practices are being proposed and put in place to curb the perceived lawlessness of the medium.

The first phase of the WSIS in Geneva (2003) ended with the adoption of two official documents: a Declaration of Principles and a Plan of Action. Controversial issues such as ICTs financing in the South and Internet Governance went under a heated debate during the preparatory process but no agreements could be reached on them. Other politically hard issues such as intellectual property rights, trade of goods and services and debt swaps were hardly addressed. The Tunis Summit, which was supposed to give an answer to unresolved issues that emerged during the first phase of the WSIS in 2003 in Geneva — in particular the democratization of the Internet governance system and the leverage of funding for the development of information and communication in the South — was closed with mixed emotions. WSIS outcomes express good intentions but in no way provides concrete mechanisms to address the disparities in access to information and communication in developed and developing countries.

In its five year history, the WSIS has failed to succeed in redressing the North-South "digital divide". Consensus in the WSIS has been elusive: the private and public sectors hold opposing views on issues such as market fundamentalism, FOSS, intellectual property rights reform, financing ICTs and Internet governance.

Technology Context for Businesses

Technology has given promise for the effective progress of businesses. Over the years technology has become innovative as well as complex. It was necessary to overcome the complexity. Technological processes were innovated to overcome the complexity. The lower cost, higher performance and advanced features of business technologies have benefited consumers.

All computing, communication and entertainment media technologies are getting integrated. The converged market is going to be intensively competitive arena with each player wanting to capture the major share of the converged market. Both our work environment and home would look completely different in next few years time or very shortly as the pace of technology shift is very fast; with all these major revolutionary technologies and convergence technologies. Looking back we would ourself wonder, how could we have lived in such primitive today's world. Long live technology!!

Therefore, *technology not only has to keep pace with changing business requirements but also out-strip them by coming up with the next big revolutionary idea*. The Internet has been hailed as the last big revolution in the technology field. What's the next big thing going to be? Turns out, we may have to wait a while for this question to be answered because, as Nilekani of Infosys says, no one knew where the iPod would spring from (2006).

According to Annaswamy MD, IBM India, one cannot wait around for the next big idea. "We believe that the real differentiator in the 21st century will be who applies technology to client problems faster and better than anyone else. *The next big thing is more about services, processes, business models or cultural innovation than just product innovation*. It will be the application of technology, and not technology itself that will help take the 10 trillion dollar worldwide IT industry and make it grow" (2006).

Service oriented architecture (SOA) — where products are being integrated with services, seamlessly across all systems, and enabled by the web — will drive the next change in transformation of businesses.

The next big growth driver lies in combining technology with business change i.e. integrated change, as many Indian companies are doing today. However, many businesses fail to achieve integrated change, which involves simultaneous changes in IT, business processes, strategy, organization and culture. Technology services will continue to play a very important role for enterprises. That sort of service hasn't been commoditized, and still yields a high premium for consulting organizations.

There is informed discussion by technology professionals about software services or the products being the next growth drivers for businesses.

Davenport Thomas (2006) points that business companies have now moved on into the space of technology-oriented services, and now the big question is whether services, too, will witness what the product side of the business went through —

commoditization. The technology-oriented services have already begun to become commoditized.

As standardization and competition drive prices downward and squeeze margins, companies will be forced to look elsewhere for the next big growth driver. According to Davenport, it used to be quite a distinction to achieve the highest level in the Capability Maturity Model (CMM) for software development, but now most major Indian software services companies have done so, and there's little differentiation to be derived from it anymore.

The answer lies in combining technology with business change, as many Indian companies are doing today. However, *many businesses fail to achieve integrated change, which involves simultaneous changes in IT, business processes, strategy, organization and culture.* That sort of service hasn't been commoditized, and still yields a high premium for consulting organizations.

Nilekani, CEO, Infosys (2006) points that Indian software services firms have only ventured into it on a small scale. Over years, different layers of technology businesses get commoditized. So it's up to companies to come up with non-commoditizable services.

There is need to develop the skills required in a technology services-led economy. This is the foundation for a new discipline that industry and academia are calling Services Sciences, Management and Engineering (SSME). This new field will bring together ongoing work in computer science, operations research, industrial engineering, business strategy, management sciences, social and cognitive sciences, and legal sciences to develop the skills required in a services-led economy.

Even within software services, there are plenty of big ideas considering that the technology integration and harnessing capabilities of companies have yet to see saturation. *Service oriented architecture (SOA) — where products are being integrated with services, seamlessly across all systems, and enabled by the web — will drive the next change in transformation of businesses.*

While product companies moving towards services was inevitable, there is inter-offer in products, which is gaining importance. It enables diverse systems to 'talk to each other', in turn, inducing cost effectiveness. Businesses have failed to achieve to make individual applications work together in a single, agile and cohesive manner. By treating various business processes as individual 'services', SOA hopes to finally resolve this thorny issue.

The fundamental business technology innovations do not happen all the time. A large part of innovation comes from incremental innovations and there are more likely to be transformational innovations than radical ones. Software applications have matured. Once 'Voice' was considered dead. But IP (Internet protocols) came in and brought VoIP, thus reviving voice through Internet. The bigger change now is that we are moving from a world of transactions to a world of interactions in a non-linear fashion. For example, in the case of iPod where the user has a series of non-linear interactions with Apple (downloads, sharing, etc) and airlines where one can print a boarding pass and get an update that the plane is delayed. *Networking, which drove transactions, will now drive interactions.*

As businesses become more and more complex, services will see constant innovation. We moved from application development and maintenance to transaction processing, and now there is infrastructure servicing. Services will not go the products way, is based on the reasoning that services differ from products since people are involved. Cultural level differentiation and global delivery models can stem commoditization. Within the services framework, there are novel ideas being implemented in the form of utility computing, where a service provider makes computing resources and infrastructure available to the customer as needed, and charges them for specific usage rather than a flat rate. Like other types of on-demand computing, the utility model seeks to maximize the efficient use of resources in order to minimize associated costs. This method is becoming increasingly common in enterprise computing, and is sometimes used for the consumer market as well — for Internet services, website access, file sharing, and other applications. *Software as a service is also gaining importance and getting users to pay as and when they use the software.* Microsoft, too, is trying to get this model in place for its products.

Meanwhile, the product model is also not ruled out completely. "Developing markets will see more of product development and research. According to NASSCOM India, there are over 175 registered companies that are involved in product development or have filed for IPRs. While larger products have been commoditized, niche products will continue to exist. Larger companies will then act as aggregators or assemblers for these niche product developers."

It is assumed that interdisciplinary use of technology will drive these businesses through another wave of success. We will see integration through interdisciplinary and cross-functional innovations. Interdisciplinary will be the way ahead and is a must for future processes. Citing the iPod as a classic example of the merger of technologies for entertainment, and entertainment along with biotechnology and nanotechnology will be the next big drivers for the industry. Nilekani (2006) points telecommunications will be a major driver of the technology business. "The world still is not on an IP network, which, once done, will deconstruct the way voice and video are sold," he says. So while there is plenty to be achieved within the industry, there are new sectors on the horizon waiting to catapult IT further. And, who knows, Microsoft may well be a biotechnology firm a decade from now.

Among the issues discussed during the international conferences in 2005 were, special and differential treatment for developing countries in the application of competition law and policy, role of economic analysis and judiciary in competition law enforcement, capacity building and technical assistance to member countries, cartels, international co-operation, and review of future work program. It has been emphasized that the principles should be developed in the form of a guide, and should not be projected as an ideal law to be mandatory imposed on all countries.

It was emphasized that more steps need to be taken to enable developing countries in dealing with international cartels and to ensure effective cooperation by the developed countries in this task, including regional cooperation. It was pointed out that the special needs of developing countries should be taken heed of and there should be special provisions and 'carve outs' for them. It was also stated that any competition law should take into cognizance the special needs of informal sectors, and the need of governments to support this sector.

Among the issues focused in 2006 and impacting global considerations were capital investments, flow of foreign funds to emerging markets, increasing oil prices and effect of Middle East wars on oil prices and supply, increase in interest rates to keep inflation under control and other factors affecting the economy of a country and thus affecting global economy and terrorism threats affecting international security. Moreover, to step up easy accessibility of communication technologies to developing countries; many initiatives were taken up by bigger technology companies like Microsoft, IBM etc. Many collaborative ventures were agreed upon to provide newer, update technologies at affordable prices such as between Google and Dell, Yahoo and Microsoft, Google and libraries and publishing houses.

Technology Diversified and Updates

The pace of technology change is fast. More and more convergence technologies are coming up and that makes a lot of difference in how we do business, how we live and even countries are governed, and the process of peace and war. Thus technologies are getting diversified and updated at a fast pace and that accelerates and facilitates the process of globalization. Technologies are diversifying, updating and in the process facilitating the businesses, its revenues are expanding and benefiting the consumers. These updates and diversifications involves the global collaboration model of research and development and mergers and acquisitions

We cite some of these updates and diversifications involving global collaboration, use and their impact in the areas of telecommunications, cellular technology, Internet VoIP, Internet security software, Internet format connectivity through high speed wireless, Computer hardware and software, data storage, digital book plan, web search and search engines. This is not a comprehensive list but a sample of what is coming up. *Handbook of Communication Models, Perspectives, Strategies* 2006 by the author presents evolutionary perspective of these technologies.

Updates in Cellular Technology

The cellular technology is being diversified and updated with different hardware and software features and technology systems from GSM to WCDMA.

Micro Technologies India Ltd. will launch LMS in global mobile market. The company has developed an innovative Global Mobile messaging product — Micro LMS (Long Messaging Service). Micro LMS fulfills the long-standing need for a messaging service that overcomes the barriers posed by a SMS (Short Message Service). It not only overcomes character limits but also enables location identification of the respective users.

While, SMS enables short messages of generally not more than 160 characters, Micro LMS enables longer messages initially limited to 800 characters. Hence, Micro LMS is more useful to transmit information service messages like news, promotional schemes and transaction statements. Another feature, which makes Micro LMS attractive, is the enabling of off-line messaging, where even if the mobile of the receiver is switched off, you can send messages to him/her, which he/she may access whenever on-line.

Micro LMS is the easier and more cost-effective option now available to mobile phone users. Application has been developed in Java (J2ME), thus it requires Java compatible handsets to run with GPRS activated SIM. This system has been recently developed by the company for the Global markets and the product has been tested live in US and other western countries and generated lot of interest.

The system benefits various sectors such as the universe of mobile phone users as well as operations involving logistics, transports, marketing, human resources and sales process within an organization, this is expected to bring in good international business with the growing mobile communication (Iris News 24th May 06).

Motorola Inc. plans to set up a plant in India to manufacture mobile devices and network infrastructure equipment, the plant is to be located near Chennai in southern India, where Finland's Nokia and Taiwan's Foxconn are building plants for telecom equipment. Motorola has tapped India's software skill base for years and employs over 2,000 engineers in development centers throughout India, including an applied research lab in Bangalore.

Bharti Airtel in India (Aug 2006) announced a strategic tie-up with Microsoft to provide the latter's Windows Mobile 5.0 platform, enabling Airtel subscribers to access corporate e-mail through direct push technology. The service will deliver powerful business applications and multimedia experience to all enterprises and SME (small and medium enterprise) customers. This new service will benefit Airtel users to access a host of Microsoft Office applications and other multimedia products on their mobile phones, besides allowing them access to corporate e-mail.

Mobile phone operators have agreed to share seven transmission towers in Delhi and two in Mumbai as part of project MOST (mobile operators shared towers initiative), which will bring down costs of setting up new towers by 50 per cent, de-clutter the city's skyline and reduce call drops. Delhi alone has nearly 6,000 cell towers, each costing nearly Rs. 30 lakh. Rapid growth in subscriber base requires expansion of telecom infrastructure, particularly towers, which are being replicated by nearly every operator. Sharing of towers will bring down infrastructure costs for all operators.

This will be the first time that GSM and CDMA operators will share the towers. In Delhi, seven towers will be shared by six service providers—Bharti Airtel, Hutch Essar, Idea Cellular, Reliance Communications, Tata Teleservices and Mahanagar Telephone Nigam Ltd. The operators under the aegis of Cellular Operators' Association of India and Association of Unified Service Providers of India will also announce plans of sharing infrastructure for the rest of the country. Infrastructure-sharing initiative was suggested in February 2006. Subsequently, a committee was formed under a joint secretary in the department of telecommunications with telecom industry representatives.

India's Minister for Communication and Information Technology supported the sharing of "passive infrastructure" like towers by telecom operators, as it would save significant resources to finance further rollouts, enhance aesthetics of the environment and lower the costs per operator.

The six cell-sites located in different parts of the national capital that were being successfully shared by mobile operators under "Project MOST" (mobile operators shared towers) was proof that the concept could be replicated in other parts of the country. "Project MOST" team had brought together GSM and CDMA operators, public and private sector players and independent infrastructure providers to establish infrastructure on a sharing basis.

"With Indian operators offering one of the lowest mobile tariffs in the world, we in India have to look at all possible solutions to improve our cost-efficiencies and offer increasingly affordable services to our customers." Shared towers would reduce the costs of the operators and the customers would be able to get quality services at affordable prices.

Shared infrastructure for mobile rollout would be launched shortly in rural areas too. For that, a detailed exercise was being undertaken to identify villages in the rural and remote areas not covered by wireless signals. With Universal Service Obligation Fund (USOF) assistance, it was proposed to create shared infrastructure to enable telecom service providers to provide cellphones in the identified rural areas. Between 8,000 and 10,000 towers were likely to be set up and this would ensure that almost 85 per cent of the area of the country was covered by wireless signal after completion of the project. Telecom operators need to extend the concept of shared passive infrastructure to rural areas (2006).

Samsung Electronics has announced the launch of its SGH-i320, a slim QWERTY Smart phone, signaling the company's foray into the smart phone market. The company claims that the i320 is perfect for users who want to have all of the advanced features of a smart phone, together with style and convenience. According to the company, the new mobile is especially useful for users who want to chat, read, and send e-mails from their mobiles. The i320 features an embedded instant messaging program, and "mobile mail" functions to allow users send and receive photos, music, and a variety of multi-media messages.

Updates in Internet

Internet Telephony needs a new device to make it safe. More and more telephone companies' world wide are offering Internet telephony. This is much cheaper. The creator of a well-known tool for keeping e-mail safe from prying eyes is now working on a program that he says will help stop eavesdroppers from listening in on Internet-based phone calls. Phil Zimmermann, who created the Pretty Good Privacy program for encrypting e-mail traffic, planned to demonstrate a prototype of his voice over Internet Protocol security program. Most Internet-based phone calls are sent unscrambled, meaning it's possible for anyone to intercept the traffic and eavesdrop. Zimmermann's application scrambles the data until it reaches its destination. The recipient must be running a program using the same protocols. "If you want to have an encrypted call, then you have to call someone running the same software at the other end," Zimmermann said "Eventually, the companies that make VoIP phones will incorporate this protocol into their phones."

ZyXEL Communications has announced the availability of its new P-2602R/RL-DxA Series ADSL2+ VoIP Internet Access Device (IAD). According to the company, the new series—including six different models, is designed for end-users to have high-speed Internet access while enjoying VoIP applications.

Austin Huang, development manager — market, ZyXEL Communications, Taiwan, said, "With intelligent Quality of Service (QoS) management features on the P-2602R/RL-DXA series, network administrators can allocate network resources effectively, to ensure quality-of-service for time-sensitive applications (such as VoIP and video-on-demand). This also prevents other bandwidth-hungry applications, such as FTP and file-sharing, from hogging network bandwidth" (July 2006).

The Nokia 770 is basically Wi-Fi connected Linux computer. Nokia designed it to be a portable internet-browsing machine. And the latest update to the operating system running on this device comes with support for voice over IP and the SIP protocol. As a result, users of this device can use it as a VoIP phone whenever they land at Wi-Fi hot spots. The OS on this tablet now comes loaded with the Google Talk application, which has both instant messaging and VoIP capabilities. And in a short time, a client for the Gizmo Project phone, by SIPP phone, will be available shortly to make calls to regular phones possibly using the Nokia 770 (July 06).

TELES India, a telecommunication manufacturer, has launched TELES.iPBX, a multifunctional and scalable Soft PBX for IP telephony controlled by SIP and H.323 protocol. It allows organizations to add extensions in local LAN, at branch offices or at home office using the Internet. TELES.iPBX provides comprehensive PBX functions to SMBs enabling them to leverage the power of IP and VoIP. The solution provides advanced least cost router mechanism to optimize cost savings and the voice network efficiency. The TELES.iPBX supports SIP and H.323 protocol providing the better utilization of IP bandwidth with complete security. It can extend the network with additional voice features, which is normally available with big PBX systems and provides n-way conferencing, IVR, call attendance, voice mail and call forwarding.

Security software makers, Microsoft Corp. was to announce that it is releasing software that aims to better protect people who use its Windows operating system from Internet attacks. The move pits the world's largest software maker head-to-head with longtime business partners Symantec Corp., McAfee Inc. and others. Windows Live OneCare, marks the latest step in Microsoft's effort over the years to make its operating system less vulnerable to crippling Internet attacks. Microsoft is hoping to gain an edge against Symantec and others by also including tools in OneCare to make computers run more smoothly and help people back up data. McAfee said that it was preparing to release a new security service, code-named Falcon in summer 2006.

Intel investing $600 millions in Clearwire is a provider of wireless, high-speed Internet services, based on WiMAX. The moves are aimed to accelerate the development and deployment of WiMAX in the marketplace. Clearwire has launched wireless high-speed Internet service in 27 metro markets, covering more than 200 cities and towns. "Collaborating with Intel and Motorola significantly advances our vision for fixed, portable and mobile wireless broadband services," said McCaw, founder, chairman, and co-CEO of Clearwire, in a statement. "Wireless broadband networks will enable the creation and delivery of differentiated services and applications that enhance the way people communicate and experience the Internet." Motorola will supply wireless broadband equipment for Clearwire's existing and future networks. To speed up the proliferation of mobile WiMAX in PC clients, Intel will work to enable the inclusion of WiMAX chipsets in next generation mobile computing platforms. All three parties will contribute research and development resources to evolve NextNet Wireless' pre-WiMAX technologies.

Search giant Google has revived its plans to set up a server farm in India. The $1-billion back-office, its second facility in India and seventh globally, is likely to be located in Andhra Pradesh, industry sources said. Google's proposal to set up a server farm in India comes amidst a surge in the number of Internet users in the country. A local server will allow users to access the internet faster and also save on accesses costs from international locations when volumes increase. Google's server farm in India will also boost the country as a preferred destination for competing companies like Microsoft and Yahoo!.

Server farms host websites and also act as a storehouse for all information available on the internet. It will store e-mails, blogs, photos, documents and chat records, and make it available to users when they demand it. Google's earlier plan to set up a server farm in the country was thwarted by infrastructure bottlenecks. Google then went to Taiwan instead to build its farm. The California-based company was in the news recently over its plans to set up an SEZ in India.

Microsoft is planning a big push into unified communications. It brings a grand vision covering VoIP, instant messaging, audio-conferencing, video-conferencing, and e-mail. Built primarily on new versions of current products, the combination of new and renamed products is intended to appeal to enterprise IT types who want to bring all of their company's communications under a single umbrella. It announced integrated software intended to turn the upcoming Office 2007 into a platform for unified voice, e-mail, IM and video communications. The company will also introduce new products including a so-called soft-phone, an application that acts like a regular telephone.

"Unified communications will drive the next major advancement in individual, team and organizational productivity in today's 24x7, always-connected and increasingly mobile work environment," Microsoft Business Division president Jeff Raikes said. "We believe that through software, we can transform business communications (bringing down both its cost and complexity) by now integrating voice communications with the familiar and powerful communications and collaboration experiences provided by Microsoft." He named six clients, server and device products plus alliances with Hewlett Packard, Motorola and Siemens as part of a carefully coordinated event in San Francisco, California, to state its vision (May 06).

As unified communications from individual devices and services, users can expect a single voice mail box for both their office and mobile phones. Microsoft also demonstrated a feature that gives users access to their calendar through a voice response system and make changes to existing appointments. The company also plans to unveil the Microsoft 'Office Round Table service'. It enables video meetings through the use of a new collaboration device, a 360-degree camera and voice directed microphones that allow it to automatically zoom in on the person speaking. It has released 'hosted Beta version of Office 2007' so that users can test drive the application without downloading and installing the software. The company released a Beta 2 of Office 2007 in May 06 and has logged over 2.5 million downloads. The final product is slated for release early next year.

With the test drive you can try out the latest improvements to familiar Microsoft Office applications and use sample data that you can edit, send by e-mail, and post to Microsoft Share Point Products and Technologies sites in real time. The online version offers access to all the Office 2007 applications as well as 18 product specific tutorials. The service is available in English from May 06. Versions in French, German, Japanese and Spanish will follow later this week. The forthcoming suite offers a radically new user interface which adapts to the task that a user is performing.

The 2007 Microsoft Office system can help you better manage documents, organize your workload, and collaborate with co-workers—not just from your desk, but from almost anywhere. Featuring in Microsoft's plans for later this year and 2007 is the Office Communications Server 2007 featuring Session Initiation Protocol (SIP) for presence-based VoIP call management, audio, video, and web-conferencing and IM within existing applications, plus Microsoft Exchange Server 2007 unified messaging that will provide a single inbox for email and voice messages along with a speech-based attendant.

Microsoft Office Communicator 2007 will work with Office Communications Server 2007 and feature presence-based, VoIP soft-phone, enterprise-level IM and connection to external networks such as MSN, AOL and Yahoo!. These functions will be available for desktops, Windows Mobile and via the browser.

Updates in Computers

Computer technology is fast diversifying, converging and updating.

Personal Computer is here to stay. The business model that created the popularity and affordability of PC will continue to drive innovation and choice in the area of personal devices such as cell, digital players and mobile PCs. The PC is becoming important and key enabler for these new digital scenarios in every corner of the world. This is just the end of the phase 1 of this evolving technology and it is now as ubiquitous as TV or automobile. It is continuing to expand its global reach, deliver new capabilities, more choices, and new opportunities to more and more people in every part of the day.

Since the dawn of the PC era, this relevance has been fueled by a technology framework that enables any PC maker in any corner of the world to design, build and market its own products based on industry-standard components and software. This technology framework also provides industry-standard ways of connecting all kinds of devices from computer mouse and keyboards to digital cameras and MP3 players.

Beside this availability and affordability business model, we would have never dreamed of a billion connected users in mere 25 years; nor would we have made the vision real of a computer at every desk and in every home in so many parts of the world. PC will be even more important in years ahead. This is because the peripheral devices and the personal computer exist in a symbiotic relationship. Together, they provide greater freedom, choice, flexibility and affordability for our options for communicating, accessing information, experiencing entertainment where and how we want. PC has expanded beyond its original use of creating documents and spreadsheets. Today, we use it as communication device, a radio, TV, movie-theater or a photo-album. It has also become an essential business tool to access World Wide Web and all that information and services that reside there through Internet. Every year, every month new innovations in hardware and software are unveiled and that ensures the enduring relevance of PC.

(BillGates of Microsoft & Paul Otellini of Intel 15th May 06 News item)

IBM management said it plans to use the larger budget to expand IBM's presence in Bangalore, India's technology hub, and build various new software labs and technology centers to develop products and offer client services. "That investment will ensure that we make the most of the opportunities to grow this marketplace, while it also enables IBM to fulfill its vision to become a globally integrated company." Standard and Poor's Equity Research analyst Megan Graham-Hackett said that, out of IBM's various investment plans for India, the more potentially attractive area of investment is the new Global Delivery Research & Development program, which aims to create a "virtual" services delivery network. Graham-Hackett said the program could offer scale without requiring new resources. In the meantime, she remained cautious on prospects for IBM's increased investment in India, noting that prior investments there have "met varying degrees of success to date."

Intel new chips Woodcrest Xeon 5100 series. While the battle for the server market continues with Advanced Micro Devices (AMD), Intel plans to introduce Xeon 5100 chips designed for the desktop and laptop markets in July and August 2006. The new processor line is based on Intel's new core Micro-architecture which promises platform advances including improved power management capabilities, more intelligent catching and memory options and an increase in the number of tasks that can be run in parallel. Intel said its new Xeon Processor 5100 for server computers is designed to run faster and use less power than other microprocessors.

The new chip is seen as strategically important not only to Intel's business, but also to its perceived role as the leading innovator in the chip industry. AMD has scored a string of key victories in recent years with its Opteron server, which many customers say is fundamentally different from—and by many measures better than—competitive Intel chip designs. With the release, Intel is targeting the sweet spot of volume servers, workstations, communications, storage and embedded markets.

For years, each company sought to beat the other in a sprint to see which one's chips could run fastest. But then AMD switched to a new design philosophy, aimed at getting computing work done more efficiently. AMD's chips also have paid a closer eye to power consumption. The more power a chip consumes, the more expensive it is to run, and the more difficult to cool. AMD's power-consumption advantage has been the source of a marketing push by AMD to make light of its competitor (BusinessWeek.com, 5/3/06).

Now new transparent microchip is the latest innovation, though it will take another five years to put it to commercial use.

Samsung Electronics has reportedly begun mass production of GDDR4 (series four of graphics double-density-rate memory), which the company claims to be the world's fastest graphics memory. Samsung says that GDDR4 processes images 33 per cent faster than the fastest memory in the market today. Graphics memory is installed on desktop PCs, notebooks, and work-stations to move huge volumes of video images simultaneously. According to Samsung, GDDR4 offers dramatically increased performance while greatly reducing power consumption. The GDDR4 uses JEDEC (Joint Electron Device Engineering Council) approved standards for signal noise reduction, including data bus inversion and multi-preamble specifications, to help attain the highest possible speed.

Marketing Director — graphics memory and mobile DRAM, Samsung Semiconductor, said, "With GDDR4-based systems, we are entering a new frontier with life-like movements and richly-textured imagery far better than the DVD movies being viewed today. Using 80-nanometer production technology, the memory has an ultra-high speed data processing rate of 2.4 Gigabits per second (Gbps)" (July 06).

A major breakthrough in Random Access Memory (RAM) by Austin based Freescale semiconductor in July 06 is pushing the limits of data storage to unseen limits and bringing a solution to a problem that has lasted in the IT industry for more than a decade.

The availability of the world's first magneto-resistive random access memory (MRAM) of its kind, winning the race to commercialize a technology that has until now been confined to the R&D labs of various firms. The Austin, Texas-based company has begun the production and sales of MRAM in volume quantities. The debut chip, named MR2A16A, is a

4 Mbit (512 KB) device that offers a combination of features and performance previously available only in separate memory technologies.

MRAM is faster than most other types of computer memory. Freescale's chip promises to read or write data in 35 nanoseconds. In addition, the most important improvement the MRAM is its capacity to store data while powered down. The new chip combines both the endurance and long life-span of the common RAM from today and the ability to keep information on its microcircuits active, without electricity passing through it. The latter represents a major breakthrough in the hardware industry for many IT giants like IBM, Toshiba or NEC.

Proponents say it could replace both flash memory, used inside cellphones and cameras, and DRAM, employed inside computers to shuttle data to the processor. Magneto-resistive RUC will enable the development of new classes of electronic devices by allowing for smaller form factors, lower cost, greater power consumption and enhanced system performance. Freescale said that the memory would find applications in gaming, networking, security and data storage. With the commercialization of MRAM, Freescale is the first-to-market a technology of tremendous possibilities and profound implications (July 06).

It's called a "BrainGate" and sounds like science fiction — a microchip implanted in the brain that helps patients paralyzed from spinal cord injuries control objects with their thoughts. The microchip connects to the area of the brain that controls movements. When a patient thinks about turning up the volume on a television, the chip collects the brain's electrical signals and transfers them to a computer. That computer then translates the signals and operates the device. It was developed by Cyberkinetics Neurotechnology Systems Inc. in Massachusetts.

Toshiba released on June 2006 a 2.5-inch, double-platter hard drive that it said features the highest density yet of any such component. The disk uses perpendicular magnetic recording technology to hold 277.1 megabits per square millimeter, or 178.8 gigabits per square inch. This density surpasses the current record, which Toshiba also holds, at 133 gigabits per square inch. The drive itself is designed to hold 200GB. Mass production of the disks will begin in August 2006. The new technology may play a role in Toshiba's planned digital audio player to be developed in conjunction with Microsoft and Japan's NTT DoCoMo for the Japanese market (IDG News Service).

Microsoft announced the creation of the Open XML Translator project, so its Office suite will support the Open Document Format (ODF) standard. The move comes in response to government requests for Microsoft products to be compatible with ODF, such as the national governments of Belgium and Denmark, and the state government of Massachusetts. The company said the next edition of Office 2007, now expected early next year—will include menu options for XML, ODF and Adobe Systems' PDF formats. The ODF support would include Office's three main formats, namely Word, Excel and PowerPoint (July 06).

Microsoft has released a new add-on for Windows XP, which allows users to create a private folder to store sensitive data. It's a useful tool for you to protect your private data when your friends, colleagues, kids or other people share your PC or account (July 06).

Updates in Data Storage

Microsoft and Intel are supporting the next generation of data storage format— HD-DVD countering the rival format Blu-ray. This is differing support for new generation technology for DVD players and discs. Earlier there were differing formats for videotapes, (PAL, Secam) CDs and current generation DVDs. These rival formats have been confusing and alienating the consumer.

Microsoft Xbox cofounder J. Allard and his team are working on Argo's development, and it will feature Wi-Fi capabilities to allow users to download content wirelessly. The Wi-Fi device will not only compete with Apple's iPod, but it will also take on wireless video game devices from Sony and

Nintendo that feature media players, Web terminals and communication mechanisms (July 06).

Apple Computer, producer of the iPod digital music and video player, decided to stop using cathode-ray-tube (CRT) monitors within its full product line, making it one of the first major computer manufacturers to offer only flat-panel monitors or displays (July 06).

HP launched miniature wireless chip with high storage capacity. HP has announced the development of a miniature, wireless data chip, which is capable of providing broad access to digital content in the physical world (July 2006).

'Memory Spot', a research team at HP Labs, has developed this memory device based on CMOS (a widely used, low-power integrated circuit design). The chip is just about the size of a grain of rice or smaller (2 mm to 4 mm square). These chips can be fixed on a sheet of paper or stuck to any surface, and the company says, it will eventually be made available as a booklet with self-adhesive dots. Some of the potential applications of this device include storage of medical records on a hospital patient's wristband; provision of audio-visual supplements for postcards and photos; help in the pharmaceutical industry's fight against counterfeit; beefing-up of identity card and passport security; and supply of additional information for printed documents. The chip has a ten megabits-per-second data transfer rate, which is ten times faster than Bluetooth wireless technology, and comparable to Wi-Fi speeds, giving users instant retrieval of information in audio, video, photo, or document form. With a storage capacity ranging from 256 kilobits to 4 megabits in working prototypes, the device can store a very short video clip, several images, or dozens of pages of text.

Digital book Plans practices have changed the way how readers access books on line. Earlier e-books plans did not work with the consumers. The best thing is to have a healthy market with several ways to access the digital material. Google print is exploring new access models to help publishers and authors to sell more books online. Google suggests a program for consumers to 'rent' on line copy of new books for a week. The book will not be downloadable or printable. It gives the publishers to tap the budding digital-book market. Google through its print library project is scanning millions of books from five universities and public libraries and letting consumers search their texts by key phrases. This has prompted backlash from publisher community. Several options are being suggested and worked out.

Several companies have announced plans to enable users to pay for the right to view books on a page-per-view basis. For example, Random house intends to sell the contents of its books on the basis with the provision that the material won't be downloadable. Authors will share the proceeds.

Amazon.com has announced two programs; One, Amazon pages will enable users to buy a page, a section, a chapter of a book to read on line for a few cents per page. In addition it intends to enable people who buy the book to access online copy of it by additional fee. Both programs are designed to respect copyrights, new revenue streams for authors and publishers.

Such efforts are aimed at expanding the audience of the books and revenue generated from them. Moreover, publishers want to be sure that rental programs supplements the physical sale of books rather than cannibalize them.

Updates in Engineering

An engineering marvel, China's newly opened 710-mile stretch of rail, linking the ancient Tibetan capital of Lhasa to a station that had been a final stop on China's vast rail network, is an unparalleled engineering marvel.

The $4.2 billion project was built in four years on delicate permafrost, marshy ground easily damaged by human encroachment. Engineers used sunshades and high-tech cooling columns plunged into embankments to help ensure the ground stays frozen. China has earmarked $190 million for environmental protection along the railway.

Chinese state media says the railway will help double tourism revenues in Tibet by 2010 and cut transport costs for goods by 75 per cent. Goods going to and from Tibet have been trucked over mountain highways that often are blocked by landslides or snow, making trade prohibitively expensive. Rail line will ensure safe passengers, cargo and military. *Political circles and activists are concerned about whether Tibetian independent identity will be submerged in Chinese politics and culture.*

Updates in Web Search

Different large Search Engines like Google, Microsoft and Yahoo are in competition to diversify and update their software technologies to provide better search facilities to consumers, expand their audience and generate more revenue. More and more search functions and capabilities have been updated recently in 2005-6 to improve performance by these search engines as they got more and more competitive. The success of any engine is how relevant are the results returned to the users' queries. It is secondary how many pages it searches. Three most popular scoped search features are Web, News and Images. These search engines are getting into personalized recommended news stories, and alerts on search interest topics. These large search engines are providing it in many languages and through a few country-based services like India, China.

All these search engines are getting into online advertising in a big way. It generates revenue for the search engines, it provides expanding audiences for the advertisers and to the consumer the relevant and related advertised product and services which he/she may not be looking currently but creates awareness, interest for the future. Google Ad sense facilitates online advertising.

The search engines suggests updates information through interaction, like Google Map helps in identifying locations, from street address to restaurants etc. The focus is on content relevance and it is provided in many languages.

Google Earth has emerged as a cause for concern — this time from a different quarter — the Indian Space Research Organization (ISRO). The bone of contention is that Google Earth allows users access to high resolution images of several "sensitive" areas, including national defense headquarters, airfields, etc.

Google should not display fine details of these areas in the interest of global security. Sources in the IAF claim that detailed images, like the manner in which aircrafts are parked, can be exploited by enemy forces to extract information on the number and status of aircrafts with the force. This is not the first time that concern has been raised over Google Earth. Earlier, several other countries including South Korea and Thailand have all voiced similar concerns.

The use of AJAX helps in better delivery of products. Ajax isn't a technology. It's really several technologies, each flourishing in its own right, coming together in powerful new ways. Ajax incorporates: standards-based presentation using XHTML and CSS; dynamic display and interaction using the Document Object Model; data interchange and manipulation using XSLT; asynchronous data retrieval using XMHLTP Request; and Java Script binding everything together.

The other major initiative at Google is the introduction of yet another advertising program. Google Content-Targeted Advertising expands the reach of the advertising beyond search engine results (what it has offered for a while now—the text ads at the top and in the right-hand margin that are labeled as "sponsored links") to placing those ads on non-search related pages on other Web sites. These text ads are starting to appear on content sites.

Searching the web isn't just about providing a long list of web links but connecting you to the answers and information you're looking for. To help with this, the new MSN Search includes a new search engine, index and crawler; all built from the ground up on Microsoft technology. With this new service, you'll be able to find faster what you're looking for. Web Search Help, Toolbar Help, Web Search SDK (Beta) are some of the new features.

Search Builder and advanced search options are other features. Use Search Builder to focus your search by adding or excluding search terms, or by limiting your search to one or more domains, countries/regions, or languages. Most advanced searches can be easily performed by using Search Builder. As you define your search terms in Search Builder, Search Builder builds a query string using a set of symbols and keywords. You can build your own advanced query strings manually by using MSN supported set of keywords and symbols.

The search module 'My Web 2.0' unveiled by Yahoo India, enables users to save, organize and tag actual web pages and bookmarks on a personal account and recall them from any computer. The module, helps users to save the search results in a personalized 'My Web' account and enables them to share their results with friends and a broader community of people with similar interests.

My Web 2.0 creates a personal online web archive for a user by saving his favorite pages, search results, and history to his personal account. The user can save, organize and find pages in a sequential manner making it easier to organize the saved pages. The search module also makes the contents of the saved web page searchable.

My web helps users tap into the power of communities, using tagging and sharing to improve their search experience

These three search engines are updating and introducing various new features in search facilities. The Internet is becoming more community-orientated and users want access to trusted information. We see social search as the next phase of web search.

Yahoo and Microsoft announced the interoperability of their IM clients, Yahoo Messenger and Windows Live Messenger. It's not really breaking news, since the interoperability was planned a year ago, when Microsoft and Yahoo accepted to cooperate in the IM domain, for the benefit of their clients. Yahoo and Microsoft stated that they have built a software bridge between their popular IM applications, thus allowing the creation of the world's largest IM and social community. In their combined press release the two companies mentioned that this community reaches more than 350 million IM accounts, now merged together due to interoperability.

An initial Beta testing session for the new feature of both Yahoo Messenger and Windows Live Messenger will be available in Argentina, Australia, Brazil, Canada, China, France, Germany, Hong Kong, India, Italy, Korea, Mexico, The Netherlands, Singapore, Spain, Taiwan, Turkey, the UK and the US (July 06).

Low-cost rural ATM with biometric sensor in India. Grammteller, a low-cost ATM machine, developed by the Telecommunications Network (TeNet) Group of IIT, Chennai is being tested in the metropolis at two places. The kiosk–ATMs are aimed at the rural market of India. The special feature of the ATM is, unlike the PIN numbers log-in access facility, it is equipped with biometric sensor so that once the customer's fingerprints are registered, PIN need not be used. The low-cost ATM makes it more user-friendly for people in rural India who are more into 'finger impression' mindset for taking cash.

Convergence: ICTs

Yoffie (2006) points that the sudden arrival of digital convergence has turned the tech world upside down. Digital convergence has arrived, creating entirely new products, services, and collaboration opportunities. The technology industry is tilting to horizontal. Players need to learn to complement each other as well as compete. Network effects create strong market advantages for companies that can capitalize on them.

He sees much of the technology business tilting horizontally. Take the future of semiconductors, for example. The dominant chip companies have traditionally been vertically integrated: Intel did (and does) its own R&D, design, fabrication, and distribution of its products and technologies. But now in the horizontal model, smaller competitors are sustaining themselves on discrete pieces of the business. "The key strategic question is where to play in the value chain; very few firms can be successful along the entire vertical chain in a converging world. In the course, we try to dissect where, and under what conditions, you want to focus on horizontal layers in the value chain versus offering fully integrated solutions," says Yoffie. The horizontal world also poses challenges for companies that are building products using parts, technologies, and services from outside vendors. "The challenge is that when multiple technologies are integrated into products and services, companies are forced to manage, develop, and/or integrate technologies beyond their traditional spheres of competence."

ICTs Scenario

The challenge is searching for the best initiatives that accelerate the use of information technology for social and economic benefit of citizens and communities in public administration, culture, health, education, economic development, and environment. These challenges call for changing communication practices. It projects the endeavors for progress in related field and better connectivity. The objective is to help local entrepreneurs, who work to close the digital divide, by bringing in research communities, development organizations and strong corporate initiatives. It is equally challenging how ICTs facilitate information and information flow democratically. That is where the concerns for digital divide develop.

Three fundamental models that help explain the role of ICTs in socio-economic development: i) role of information; ii) context; iii) supply and demand. Increased effectiveness of development efforts with local relevance is assessed through these three models.

The growing gap — with a few emerging nations including China and India bucking the trend — contradicted conventional wisdom that income differences would close as the world economy became more integrated, the UN's "World Economic and Social Survey 2006: Diverging Growth and Development," report.

The digital content from each country should promote the development of an "Information Society." It should aim not only to make the benefits of the new "Information Society" accessible and meaningful for all humanity, but in particular to raise public awareness and give deserved public recognition to the highest quality e-Content produced all over the world. The following eight categories of content are focused: e-Learning; e-Culture; e-Science; e-Government; e-Health; e-Business; e-Entertainment; and e-Inclusion.

New practices are emerging in use of ICTs for ***higher education***. The key issues related to the use of ICT in higher education explores the concept of open course content, its context, current initiatives, and issues and implications of its use. Open course content – course elements and materials that are freely available on the Internet for consultation, use and adaptation – constitutes an important resource to higher education institutions. However, if there is little or no awareness of availability, it cannot be exploited, and even with awareness of availability, there are challenges and barriers to its effective use.

Organizing a series of activities to increase awareness, and support capacity building and informed decision making related to the provision and use of openly available course content is needed.

Information Technologies and International Development (ITID) is a leading MIT Press journal that focuses on the intersection of information and communication technologies (ICTs) with international development. It addresses the issues how universities in developing countries are implementing innovative teaching, research and outreach activities that link ICTs to the development-related needs and activities of different local and national stakeholders, including scientists, educators, entrepreneurs, governments, civil society organizations, and rural communities.

It reflects how universities in developing countries are seeking to contribute to 'ICT for Development' efforts, the impact of their efforts upon society and universities, and the internal and external challenges they face in realizing a productive and meaningful place in the ICT for development movement.

The focus has not only to be on building universities' ICT capacity, but on their capacities to leverage ICTs to foster social and economic development.

For example, some relevant topics could be (a) the institutional capacity of universities to create knowledge tailored to different outside stakeholders; (b) the uses and effects of university involvement in community projects such as telecenters; (c) the creation of university programs that prepare students to become professionals in ICT-enabled development; or (d) efforts by universities to engage in local, national, or international policy-relevant research on emerging ICT issues.

New practices in ***e-learning*** suggest broader deployment of conferencing technology in class rooms, to incorporate conferencing technology and other technologies into courses of study. This has made e-learning more effective. This is happening as there is technology improvement, enhanced functionality, lower pricing and increasing demand for e-learning solutions. Today's 'media conferencing' approach is integrating audio, video and multimedia tools enabling the use of power point and other desktop applications teaching used in teaching environment now that is available in video-conferencing. The increased functionality, combined with intuitive easy to understand user interfaces, makes it simple for educators to adopt new technology in classroom settings. Even the conference equipment vendors are offering customized solutions that fit educational needs. Manufacturers have moved away from proprietary systems to standards-based equipments and are incorporating PC functionality.

E-governance creates democracy of communications through democratization of technology. ICTs are deployed for e-governance. Different countries have different guidelines for it depending upon when they are ready for it politically as well technologically and find it financially viable. The e-governance practices change accordingly. It is important that both government functionaries and citizens focus should be tech savvy. It is equally important that e-governance technology should be physically and socially accessible, and financially viable for governments and affordable for the citizens.

India has been experimenting with e-governance with some initial headway. Some of its practices are targeted at central government administration, municipal administration in cities and rural administrative blocks and village panchyats and citizenry in general.

The slow progress was due to low computer literacy, low accessibility of computers and low tele-density in urban and rural areas. With improved tele-density by cellular phones and community computers, many e-governance projects and practices are targeting the rural areas for better governance.

In early 2006 in India, the Department of Information Technology (DIT) has issued guidelines for capacity building and institutional framework for e-governance under the National E-Governance Plan (NEGP) and called for a program steering council to provide the overall vision and broad policy direction. The government intends that at least one in six villages should be covered by e-governance, making the civic-related procedures easier and simpler. As per the mandate of the Department of Administrative Reforms and Public Grievances, all the central ministries and departments should have a website of their own.

Digital Divide: Technology Bridges

Digital Divide can be viewed from four perspectives: access, ability to use, actual use and the economic returns of the ICTs used. These are explained as, i) A gap in access to use of ICTs—broadly measured by the number and spread of telephones or web-enabled computers. ii) A gap in the ability to use ICTs—measured by the skills base and the presence of numerous complimentary assets. iii) A gap in actual use—the minutes used of telecommunications for various purposes, the number of users and amount of time used online, the number of Internet hosts, and the level of electronic commerce. iv) The impact and economic returns of use of ICTs.

But, despite the reported rapid adoption of ICT into administration, education and several sectors of the economy, the greatest challenge still remains; how can ICTs be demystified to appeal to the majority of the local population who still view them as tools designed for the minority elite.

In whatever human trait you view Information Communication Technologies (ICTs), most people have widely accepted that it plays a key role in shaping the social economic development of any society. But the technical nature and the complexities involved in understanding ICTs tools have created the digital divide between the developed countries and the third world nations; rural and urban segments and between the have and have-nots in the society.

Much attention has focused on the digital divide in developing countries as an issue of lack of access to ICTs. The answers to bridging the gap, however, involve much more than basic Internet access. The key to unlocking ICTs for development involves a focus on a range of parameters which can be referred to as the *8 Cs of the digital economy: connectivity, content, community, commerce, capacity, culture, capital and cooperation* (Rao, 2002). In other words, it is important to have affordable and widespread access to ICTs, locally relevant content in local languages, offline and online forums for discussing ICT applications, e-commerce services, and human resource capacity, a culture which embraces innovation, investment capital, and cooperation between multiple stakeholders.

Digital divide can occur in areas and functionality in telecommunications, computers, use of Internet, higher education, agriculture development, e-development etc. Both national and international efforts are made to bridge the digital divide to certain extent.

Despite the positive benefits telephony can have for economic development, many people in developing nations are held back by a diverse set of factors — such as low connectivity in rural locations, duties and taxes imposed by governments, the costs of handsets and the cost of services. Once the hurdle of access to communication is overcome, people in developing nations still have to contend with the costs of services. Usage costs can play a large role in determining the purposes for which, and the frequency with which, people use their phones.

It is often claimed that access to telecommunication facilities is a propeller of economic prosperity in developing countries. Mobile phones in particular are considered pivotal in encouraging growth. Prahlad (2004), in *Fortune at the Bottom of the Pyramid asserts that defining change in the world's poorest economies will be led by access to* communications and not through the evolution of IT as was the case in the advanced *countries of the world.* A study by the London Business School has also found that, in a typical developing country, an increase of 10 mobile phones per 100 people would boost GDP growth by 0.6 percentage points (Waverman et al., 2005).

SIDA is mobilizing Sweden's ICT resources to bridge the digital divide in the world. SPIDER, the Swedish Program for Information and Communication Technology in Developing Regions aims at reinforcing the Swedish support activities in the field of information and communication technology (ICT) in developing countries. It is a national centre that mobilizes Sweden's ICT resources. SPIDER is supported by SIDA and hosted by the Royal Institute of Technology, KTH, in Kista, Stockholm. Spider's main task is to pull together all ICT resources, related to sustainable development, in Sweden, and make them available to developing countries. The Centre acts as a meeting place and a catalyst for ICT experts and entrepreneurs, who are interested in strengthening their commitment to the UN millennium Development Goals.

Developing nations require the education, Internet connectivity and the access to the right technology to meet their unique needs. Intel, Microsoft, IBM and other technology companies are trying to bridge the digital divide among the rural and lower socio-economic population in developing countries through ambitious programs. *These are the next steps for developing Information Society among the poor and rural population by bridging the digital divide.*

'World Ahead' program, of Intel aims to bridge digital divide. Intel is working with governments worldwide to develop innovative, cost-effective programs that increase access to PCs and the Internet, improve educational outcomes, grow local ICT industries and develop the skills and infrastructure that nations, citizens and businesses need to thrive. Intel pledges to invest $1 billion over the next five years to broaden access to technology — computers and Internet access, and educational resources in developing countries. Intel and Advanced Micro Devices Inc are experimenting to bring inexpensive hardware and Internet connections to underdeveloped regions.

The program has three primary goals: to design affordable computers tailored to the needs of the developing countries; to make high-speed Internet access more ubiquitous in some cases by use of WIMAX technology; and to provide training to teachers and students on the use of information technology.

Intel is working with governments and telecommunication companies in the regions to design computer system that would start around $300 each. Other companies have also proposed simpler PC or terminals costing less.

Intel's through its community computer initiative in India is providing low cost PC in rural India. In March (2006) it unveiled a prototype PC for use in India where dust, heat, and humidity can cause reliability problems. This PC can withstand these. Given the electricity problems in rural India, it can run on alternate power sources including a car battery. Another prototype of a full featured computer notebook is expected to cost less than $400. It has started an initiative 'jagruti' (awakening) in coordination with this technology donation of community PCs to help bridge the digital divide. It could have the advantage of exposing children to technology at an early age. It opens up whole range of opportunities for the villagers. Intel sees potential in India and its talented pool of citizens. Intel is now working with Indian manufacturers Wipro and HCL technologies to produce these computers.

As part of World Ahead Program (WAP), Intel plans to donate 100,000 PCs for use in classrooms in developing nations. The company has already been spending 100 million a year on educational programs. It has trained about three million teachers so far in the use of technology, and plans to train 10 million more over five years as part of the World Ahead program.

WAP of Intel is set to chip in much more in India. Chip maker Intel will boost its India story with new initiatives planned to accelerate technology accessibility, Internet connectivity and effective education. *The initiatives, coming under this program, include low-cost computers, pay-as-you-go*

PC purchasing models, small learning devices for education and extending WIMAX broadband connectivity in the country.

The low cost, fully featured desktop PCs priced 20% lower than the current Intel configured ones will be launched in 2006 and the company will work with HCL, Millennium, PCS, Wipro and Zenith Computers for the Discover the PC initiative.

Intel has recently (2006) launched its Community PC, a flexible pay-as-you-go PC purchasing model in India. Another product set for introduction is an affordable, rugged learning device for students — code named Eduwise. The notebook to provide collaborative learning between teachers and students in developing countries was designed in Intel's Bangalore platform definition centre. We expect to launch it in the first half of '07 priced less than $400," Mr Otellini, the president and CEO of Intel said.

He said the India facility will play a key role in designing and developing computing technologies for the WAP. "The Bangalore centre, along with Intel's platform definition centers in Shanghai, Cairo and Sao Paulo, will work on specialized products for emerging markets," Mr Otellini said.

India is one of the five critical markets, Otellini, told the media in Bangalore, that "with only 2% of India's population having a PC or Internet connection, the potential for increasing PC penetration is immense and challenging. By multiplying the effects of computers, Internet and education, we intend to accelerate the reach of technology benefits in the country over the next five years."

Intel will be investing $1bn in India in the next five years to grow its R&D, venture capital activities and education and community program. So far, the company has invested about $750m.

Among other programs, In India, Intel will collaborate with ICICI Bank to facilitate loans for PC ownership through the emerging subscription payment model and working with Tata VSNL to bring Intel-based PC solutions and WiMAX wireless broadband connectivity to Tata's RailTel cyber cafes across India.

Intel will also train about 8 lakh teachers in India as part of the 10 million target it has worldwide by 2010. Since 2000, the '***Teach to the Future***' initiative has trained about 5.5 lakh teachers in the country.

The chip manufacturing plant in India is not happening too soon, going by the Intel chief's words, "I will always argue that chip design units which are knowledge intensive have much more value in short term than chip manufacturing plants. However, we are still in talks with the Indian government as they put together a package for the chip industry."

Intel will remain focused on existing business areas. In addition, it sees significant opportunities to apply their technology and innovation to new segments such as the emerging markets and healthcare. In 2006 it will bring to market dual-core processors across the desktop, notebook and server segments. Their strategy for 2006 is also focused on driving the 65-nm product ramp as fast as possible; quickly shifting chipsets to 300-mm factories on 90-nm process technology; and, ramping platforms for digital home, mobility, and digital enterprise.

What will be Intel's role in extending the benefits of technology to the next billion populations? The emerging markets will be one of their key focus areas for driving the company's growth. *While the emerging markets, including India, presents a significant business opportunity for Intel, it's also good business to act as a good global citizen.* This is one reason why they have created the Intel World Ahead Program in May 2006, which Intel plans to invest more than $1 billion globally over the next five years to speed access to uncompromised technology and education for people in the world's developing communities. What role will India have in the overall scheme of Intel? Will we see more of "created in India" products?

Intel's approach to emerging markets goes beyond simply providing low cost components. Instead, the company believes people in developing nations require the education, Internet connectivity and the access to the right technology to meet their unique needs. Through the Intel World Ahead Program, they have taken a multifaceted approach to this. They are creating customized technology solutions which enable new types of PCs that meet the specific needs of developing countries, such as the recently introduced Intel powered Community PC in India. Intel plans to develop six more geographically tailored PC designs worldwide in the next two years. These include low-cost, full-featured, easy-to-use PCs for home and work, community PCs customized for public access, PC kiosks, and low-cost PCs tailored to the needs of schools and educators.

The platform definition centers they have established around the world, including in Bangalore, will play a central role in these efforts. Intel is also continuing its efforts to grow the availability of WiMAX technology for low cost broadband access.

A changing Business communication practice for PC in developing and emerging countries is changing to create accessibility for consumers having lower income and limited access to credit. Narula (2004) highlighted that such changing practices in late 90s and 2000 decade created mobile access boom in developing countries for the lower strata of people and created social change in India. In an effort to replicate the success of prepaid mobile phones in emerging markets, the PC industry aims to expand PC use in countries where consumers must cope with a lower income and limited access to credit.

Microsoft announces new computer ownership program (2006). Microsoft, chip makers and PC firms aim to increase PC usage in the developing world with a new flexible payment program to lower the initial costs of buying a computer. Microsoft, the world's largest software maker, said it is leading a group of technology companies in offering the first-ever "pay-as-you-go" computers in Brazil, India, Mexico, Russia and China over the next several months. The pay-as-you-go model lowers the initial costs of buying a PC by 50 per cent or more and the consumer owns the PC after a set amount of minutes are purchased.

Using Microsoft's Flex Go software technology, a customer can buy a computer loaded with the Windows operating system then purchase prepaid cards powered by Microsoft Flex Go technology or pay a monthly subscription fee at a cost similar to using a computer at a local Internet cafe, Microsoft said. When the usage time ticks down, a customer can go online or to a local retailer to buy more minutes.

Microsoft's is working with partners Advanced Micro Devices, Intel, Lenovo, Phoenix Technologies and Transmeta, but it also aims to work with other hardware companies, telecommunication firms, banks and retailers in emerging markets to expand the market to help bring PCs within reach for hundreds of millions of families within emerging markets. The personal computing offer has been designed for fast emerging markets.

Microsoft on May 22, 06 in New Delhi announced this computer ownership program for India. Microsoft has entered into a tie-up with BSNL, Intel and Lenovo to provide users a complete PC under this offer in India. "The trial service of this product will be launched in June and on the basis of users' feedback, the actual product will be rolled out after 3-4 months". The company has already completed successful trials of this offering in Brazil with various industry partners. The next round of trials would look at countries such as China, Hungary, Mexico, Russia, Slovenia, Vietnam and India (Press release 2006).

Another effort: What do you do when challenged with difficult conditions that make your computer repeatedly crash in rural, tropical conditions? Fantsuam Foundation of Nigeria suggests some solutions and simply converted this into an opportunity. Computers in wooden boxes, minus spinning disks that get clogged in dust and crash in high temperatures, and desktops that consume a fraction of power other computers need is the solution.

A two-part documentary, "*The Code Breakers,*" aired on BBC World starting 10 May 2006 examines whether free/open source software (FOSS) might be the bridge for the digital divide that is getting wider.

FOSS contains 'source code' that can be used, copied, studied, modified and re-distributed without restrictions. It has been around for over 20 years but most PC owners are not aware that the Internet search engines and many computer applications run on FOSS.

"It's not that FOSS has had a bad press, it has had no press because there is no company that 'owns' it," says executive producer Robert Lamb. "But we found that in the computer industry and among the aficionados, it is well known and its virtues well understood."

The crew of the independent producers who made the film went to nearly a dozen countries around the world to see; how the adoption of FOSS presents opportunities for industry and capacity development, software piracy reduction, and localization and customization for diverse cultural and development needs.

Stories from "The Code Breakers" include computer and Internet access for school children in Africa, reaching the poor in Brazil, tortoise breeding programs in the Galapagos, connecting villages in Spain, and disaster management in Sri Lanka. The documentary also includes interviews from key figures around the world.

Intel, IBM, Sun and Microsoft all seem to agree that FOSS is a welcome presence in computer software.

According to Jonathan Murray of Microsoft, "The Open Source community stimulates innovation in software, it is something that frankly we feel very good about and it is something that we absolutely see as being a partnership with Microsoft."

Another practice that is catching up is computer networking for setting pool of computational power. What if each of the Worlds's estimated 650 million PCs could be linked to focus on solving critical real-world problems? This is what World Community Grid has set out to do. Leveraging donated idle PC time from volunteers around the world, World Community Grid establishes a permanent, flexible infrastructure that gives humanitarian researchers a readily available pool of computational power. Their Human Proteome Folding project seeks to identify the functions of the proteins that are coded by human genes, while future projects could support infectious disease research, earthquake predictions, crop yield improvement, and the evaluation of natural resource supplies. Research proposals from developing countries are welcomed, as are volunteers willing to donate their idle PC time.

Overcoming the digital divide in conjunction with other socio-economic divides will remain one of the key development issues for decades to come. Innovations in low-cost devices have yet to reach take-off stage, and the open source movement is making notable but slight inroads into the education and government sectors.

ICTs Initiatives in India

India has vast potentials for developing and harnessing ICTs; as well it faces the domestic challenges of unleashing and harnessing ICTs. As a content-rich country with a free press, an affluent, tech-savvy diasporas spread across the world, and a huge pool of cutting edge IT and design skills, India has a lot to offer the domestic and global Internet markets. But there is poor Internet connectivity outside of the major cities. Though India is still by and large a developing nation, but there is also rapidly expanding information society within. India has more information workers than Japan and the same number as in the USA.

By 2006, India has about 30 million Internet users, more than 49 million cellphone users and a tele-density of just over 3 per cent in a country with close to half the population around the poverty line. Standardization of local language fonts and keyboards has been a stumbling block for local language digital content publication, though some initiatives are beginning to make headway.

The youth — especially in urban areas — are very Net-savvy, and the gender divide is narrowing in this segment as well. In terms of employment, the IT and IT-enabled services sector in India is a rapidly expanding industry and continues to draw significant pools of talent and energy, despite the current economic downturn globally. India seems to have cemented its position as the "outsourcing centre of the world"; and Indian software, services and content companies are gearing up to move up the value chain from basic services to products. In addition to tapping the global software market, having a sizeable domestic user base means India can sustain a lot of local infrastructure, content, foreign capital investment and an online market in general — unlike other, smaller countries that need to focus much more on overseas markets.

According to Singhal and Rogers (2001), "No other nation provides a better example of the role of the new communication media in the development process through which a country moves from being an agriculture-based economy towards becoming an information society."

The digital economy of India during 2003-2004 was marked by an explosion in the cellular phone market, a boom in outsourcing, steady Internet growth, media convergence, growth in rural ICT initiatives, benchmarking with China, and regulatory stumbling blocks. As a benchmark of economic growth and ICT diffusion, it is becoming increasingly common to compare and contrast the domestic scenario in India with the corresponding environment in China. Regulatory potholes continue to hinder speedy progress on many fronts: private operator interconnectivity, VoIP, and wireless services eligibility etc.

In the ICT industry, the recent cuts in excise duty on computer hardware and cellular phones are expected to drive domestic demand for hardware. The cellular phone market has been growing steadily since the late 1990s, but in 2003 these new telephones really took off in urban areas. NASSCOM forecasted the cellular phone user base to reach 33 million in 2003-2004 and 49 million in 2005 and 82.4 million by August 2006. At the same time, Internet growth has been steady, particularly among youths and business professionals. The total number of Internet users is estimated at around 30 million. The big concern is the shortage of international bandwidth, which NASSCOM estimates will exceed 20 Gbps by mid-2005. Prices of international bandwidth are still not at par with those of neighboring countries. This could hinder Internet usage and the outsourcing business to some extent.

Research firm Gartner projected cellular phone connections in India to touch 56 million by the end of 2004, representing a steep growth of almost 96 per cent over the previous year. Driven by the introduction of full-mobility CDMA cellular services and stiff competition among GSM operators, 2004 broke all records for growth in the Indian mobile market (Rediff.com). Volatility in the cellular market was expected to continue until at least 2006 as the main operators carved out their future market positions and some other players attempted to establish their niche positions. Samsung and LG enjoy an early mover advantage, working with local operators such as Reliance. Nokia and Motorola have started to make their presence felt in the CDMA and WCDMA market.

Based on India overview in Digital Review reports Asia-Pacific 2003-4, 2005-6, Narula (2006) has pointed, the revolution in cellular phones in India has brought social change and given connectivity and business enhancement to the lowly placed in the society. This has changed the way these people communicate about themselves socially, vocationally and professionally.

India set to log in to new Internet regime. With exhaustion of Internet protocol addresses under the current technology looming large, India is set to join a select group of countries to adopt IPv6 technology, which is considered to be a long-term solution to overcome the limitations of the present IPv4 Internet regime. In addition to offering almost infinite address space, IPv6 technology is considered as the solution for end-to-end global connectivity and Internet scalability.

It can also dwarf the current network into oblivion as it can support unlimited voice over Internet protocol, grid computing, 3G, gaming, file sharing, remote sensing, ad hoc networks, mobile devices, intelligent transport systems, consumer electronics and smart homes among other applications.

However, a slew of contentious issues, including the role of the government and the licensor in the transition, are yet to be addressed. While global players such as Cisco Systems, Sun Microsystems and HP and some Indian operators are in favor of the regulator and the government playing a major role, the proposal has been strongly opposed by the Internet Service

Providers Association of India (the body representing all ISPs), Sify and MTNL.

The Telecom Regulatory Authority of India has also been entrusted to find solutions to other issues such as policy initiatives, the transition mechanism that is best suited for the migration, the requirement for a national test bed and dividing the transition cost among the stakeholders.

"The inclusion of IPv6 as a significant element of a larger national strategy on IT is of critical importance. The subject should be addressed alongside infrastructure issues such as broadband and mobile wireless," said global networking giant, Cisco Systems, in its response to TRAI on the issue.

Wipro Technologies has meanwhile said India has already been left behind in adopting the new technology. It has also pointed out that while India's software community was engaged in product development and services related to IPv6 for overseas market, the country was yet to realize this potential.

Countries like Japan, Korea and China were in the forefront along with the EU, as they had deployed research and experiment budgets for this very early on, the company said. "These countries are in the forefront only because of the government policy and regulations. If the industry is allowed to do it at its own pace, we will not be ready at the appropriate time and sudden migration could result in a shoddy job," Wipro added. On similar lines, Bharti, too has told the government that migration from IPv4 to IPv6 must be carried out in strict pre-defined time frame. "The new IP version must be implemented from a pre-decided date.

India is set to join a select group of countries to adopt IPv6 technology, which is considered to be a long-term solution to overcome the limitations of the present IPv4 Internet regime. In addition to offering almost infinite address space, IPv6 technology is considered as the solution for end-to-end global connectivity and Internet scalability. The subject should be addressed alongside infrastructure issues such as broadband and mobile wireless. Though India's software community was engaged in product development and services related to IPv6 for overseas market, the country is yet to realize this potential.

ICTs scenario in India presents lop-sided scenario, paradoxically; India still has a long way to go in making ICT widely available to its population especially in rural areas where most of India's population lives. Tele-density is 31 per cent in urban areas, rural is less than two per cent. "We must replicate urban telephony conditions in rural areas to improve rural tele-density," said Chairman, TRAI (Telecom Regulatory Authority of India). TRAI says that the rural markets should now be viewed as an opportunity rather than an obligation, and private companies can only be attracted if the government also reduces charges for the license and the spectrum. That would mean a greater use of wireless technology, rather than wiring up rural India. "It is cheaper to take mobile technology rather than wires everywhere, that is why we want to take mobile technology to rural areas rather than fixed lines," he added. Earlier years TRAI has been focusing on fixed landlines through rural exchanges which have not been a success.

TRAI says that unless these recommendations are implemented at the earliest, tele-density in rural areas is likely to remain stuck at 3-4 per cent, and Union IT and Communications Minister's dream of 250 million telephone connections and 22 per cent tele-density by 2007, will remain just a dream. Other private companies making efforts for rural telephony are Bharti in deal with Nokia for rural cellular network expansion in India. Tata Tele is to provide communications solution to expand rural mobile telephony (2006).

The changing communication practice in India to provide telephone connectivity as well increase tele-density in rural areas is through cellular technology. It is cheaper and does not require rural electrification.

India is making efforts to provide IT and IT enabled services to the lower socio-economic groups and in rural areas. This is changing the way computers are being used and these devices are changing the information processing and knowledge gain in many sectors relevant to their life and occupations. The role of new communication media in the development process through which a country moves from being an agriculture-based economy towards becoming an information society is commendable.

Government in India is making new efforts to bridge the digital divide in India through computer literacy in government run schools where majority of children are from lower status as these schools provide free education. Ministry is hoping that the third attempt to bridge the digital divide between private and government schools succeeds where the earlier two endeavors of Computer Literacy and Studies in Schools (CLASS) in the 1980's and revised-CLASS of 1990's failed (2006). Computer literacy programs are likely to benefit from Intel's World Ahead program and Teach to the Future, and Microsoft cheap computers for India programs and IBM's expanding presence in Bangalore, India's technology hub, and build various new software labs and technology centers to develop products and offer client services. These we have discussed in the earlier sections.

Overtime, there is greater realization about the widening digital divide between urban and rural segments and between men and women which is hampering the development process. There is national government and private partnership and efforts; there are also international efforts to bridge this digital divide. It is assumed ICTs will empower women particularly in rural areas; and rural segments in general will be empowered more in economy and development through ICTs accessibility. The increased focus is on tele-density, cellular phones, Internet connectivity through broadband access and wireless access, computer literacy and computer accessibility and affordability of these information technologies.

Here is projection of ICTs scenario in India based on Minister of Communication speech "Can we Bridge the Infrastructure Deficit?" The India Today Conclave 2006, (held on 11 March 2006).

Tele-density: India's overall tele-density is 12 per cent. However this is skewed. Urban rural divide is evident. Rural India is demanding more coverage and infrastructure. We have plans of 250 million lines by 2007. By 2010 India hopes to go up to 500 million. Would this eliminate digital divide? This translates into only 22 per cent of overall tele-density by 2007 and may be about 45 per cent by 2010. *The skewness of the rural urban divide will still be there.* State Wide Area Networks (SWANs) will be set up over a period of 5 years. These SWANs will extend data connectivity of 2 Mega bits per second up to the block level in State or Union Territory in the country. The block level nodes in turn will have a provision to extend connectivity further to the village level using contemporary wireless technology.

Internet access: The aim is to reduce the digital divide by providing Internet access and IT enabled services to the community at large and to facilitate citizen interface with the government by establishing 100,000 web enabled Citizen Service Centers or CSCs in rural areas, which will serve not only as the front end for most government services, but also as a means to connect the citizens of rural India to the World Wide Web. CSCs would extend the reach of electronic services, both government and private to the village level. It is these advances in ICT technologies, which have enabled the government to take concrete steps towards turning citizens' dream of "Government at your doorstep" into a reality.

Broadband Policy: There is potential of Broadband service in growth of GDP and enhancement in quality of life through societal applications including tele-education, tele-medicine, e-governance, entertainment as well as employment generation by way of high speed access to information and web-based communication, government has come out with a Broadband Policy to provide affordable services to the public. BSNL and MTNL have launched broadband services across the country and people can get access to such connections for as little as Rs. 199 a month in 2006. Airtel and other telecom companies are offering at competitive prices. We have touched a million broadband connections so far. We expect to see 20 million by 2007.

Internet Promotion: National Internet Exchange of India (NIXI) has been set up to improve the quality of service and help in efficient routing of the domestic traffic within the country. Four Internet Exchange Nodes have been set up and made operational at Noida (U.P.), Mumbai, Chennai and Kolkata, and as many as 40 ISPs have been connected with these nodes. Government has installed three mirror Internet root servers at Delhi, Mumbai and Chennai. The root servers form a critical part of the global Internet infrastructure.

Internet Content: Most of the Internet content is in English. Language is therefore an important barrier. There is increased focus on Indian languages and making packaged software available in local languages. To enable wide proliferation of ICTs in Indian languages, government has taken a major initiative to make available tools and fonts in various Indian Languages freely to the general public. It has released in the public domain, various Tamil language fonts, e-mail client, Optical Character Recognition (OCR) software, spell checker and dictionary in April 2005. Similarly, the Hindi and Telugu software tools and fonts were released in June 2005 and October 2005, respectively. Software tools and fonts in Punjabi and Urdu are ready for release. All Indian languages are expected to be covered in the next one year.

Cost: Government is making efforts to make Internet and telephones affordable to all. As a first step towards making long distance tariffs more affordable, government in May 2005 made telephone calls within States equivalent to local calls. The second step was taken in November 2005 where the government significantly reduced the entry barrier for acquiring national and international long distance licenses. On January 1, 2006, government allowed Access Service Provider to provide Internet telephony, Internet services and Broadband services. 'One India initiative' enables people to talk from Kashmir to Kanyakumari at a very affordable tariff of Re. 1 per minute. There is focus on lowering the cost of PC at below Rs.10,000. This will increase PC penetration. The fact still remains that unless content is relevant, use of ICTs will always be constrained.

Government is in the process of giving a final shape to a scheme for supporting infrastructure for roll out of cellular mobile services in the rural areas. Keeping in mind the difficult conditions in these areas, it is proposed to provide financial support for land, tower, power and electronic equipment for transmitting, receiving and backhaul. A "plug and play" scenario will be created for the telecom service providers. The emphasis will be on sharing the infrastructure so that Capex costs can be kept down and on encouraging adoption of technology which can reduce power consumption and therefore operating costs. The infrastructure thus created will be used progressively for providing broadband connectivity and will be able to accommodate equipment of new and emerging technologies.

Electronic Hardware: India has been recognized as a force to reckon within the software sector. However, a country of the size of India cannot merely subsist on software alone. It must have capabilities in Hardware. The government has identified growth of Electronics, Telecommunications and Hardware manufacturing sector as a thrust area. The government has set up a National Manufacturing Competitiveness Council (NMCC) to provide a continuing forum for policy dialogue to energize and sustain the growth of manufacturing industry including IT Hardware. BSNL and MTNL have adopted a policy that henceforth only such vendors who set up their manufacturing facilities in core areas in India will alone be able to participate and that such vendors will add at least 30 per cent value addition in India. With the spread of Information Technology (IT) and IT Enabled Services (ITES), the time is ripe to make India a preferred destination for the manufacture of semi-conductors and other high technology IT products including Wafer; Assemble, Test and Manufacture of Semi-conductors; Flat LCD/ OLED/ Plasma Panel Displays; and Storage Devices.

In 2006, many global players in telecom and IT giants have set up manufacturing and research facilities in the country. These include reputed names such as Alcatel, Aspocomm, Ericsson, Cisco, Flextronics, Foxcomm, Microsoft, Motorola, Nokia, Samsung, LG, SemIndia-AMD, Intel etc. These global telecom and IT companies have together committed investments of over USD 8 billion in hardware manufacturing or chip design or R&D or to develop software products.

***Human resource development*:** The gap in the ability to use ICTs need to be narrowed for empowerment. Here is where the HRD and capacity building comes into play. Education is the fundamental enabler of the knowledge economy. Well-educated and skilled people are essential for creating, sharing, disseminating, and using knowledge effectively. *Government is focusing on education and training in the area of IT to make available skilled and quality professionals in the specific IT domain.* Government has been very supportive in adopting broadband as an important vehicle for delivery of educational content and is planning to connect all the secondary schools and colleges in the country by Broadband.

(Based on Minister of Communication speech, "Can we Bridge the Infrastructure Deficit?" The India Today Conclave 2006, held on 11 March 2006).

ICTs and Development: Bridging the India's Digital Divide

The stories 1-8 from Indian rural and urban slum scene suggest how even simple applications of ICTs in rural communities of India are helping women and others to reap even the basic benefits of life. How by adapting these technologies to local environments and affordability, they are bridging the digital divide in accessibility, learning, and practical applications of information and knowledge gain for better living. These reflect the life situations in 2005-06.

Story 1. Various workshops by M.S. Swaminathan Research Foundation (MSSRF) in India provide an opportunity for the exchange of knowledge and perspectives between village communities in Tamil Nadu and Pondicherry in southern India and civil societies from developing countries with a specific focus on ICT-enabled development.

These action-learning workshops help participants learn about how to integrate modern ICT effectively in their development projects, provide perspectives regarding various technologies and innovations involved in rural ICT, and help participants to blend ICT in the local knowledge management process. These workshops make efforts in facilitating learning from concrete, on the ground, practical knowledge in the use of ICT for development.

***Story** 2.* For 12-year-old Anju from Bithoor, India, hope for a better life arrives in her poor farming village three days a week on a bicycle rickshaw that carries a computer with a high-speed, wireless Internet connection.

Designed like temple carriages that bear Hindu deities during festivals, the brightly painted pedal-cart rolls into her village in India's most populous state, accompanied by a computer instructor who gives classes to young and old, students and teachers alike. Conceived in 2003 by the Indian Institute of Technology in Kanpur, about 10 miles southwest of Bithoor, the project is funded by the national government and provides free computer classes in six villages here in Uttar Pradesh state.

The bicycle cart is the center of a project called "Infothela", or info-cart. It aims to use technology to improve education, health care and access to agricultural information in India's villages, where most of the country's 1.06 billion people live.

Another computer on a Pedicab is being used in an experiment to help doctors in Lucknow, the state capital, provides consultation to villagers through video-conferencing in nearby Saroha village. A project to disseminate the latest crop prices and farming methods is also being developed.

In Bithoor, on the banks of the Ganges river in northern India, manual labor is the alternative to farming and annual incomes rarely exceed $130. Sharma's teachers make only $11 a month. Young people look for jobs in cities, but often lose out to better educated urbanites. Computers and Internet will open up new opportunities for these villagers.

With only 12 computers and 4 Internet connections per 1,000 people, India has one of the world's lowest Internet usage rates and much of rural India remains oblivious to the sweep of technology. But all the villages involved in Infothela and Pedicab projects lie within a 50-mile wireless corridor created by the Institute of Technology and linked by high-rise Wi-Fi antennae and amplifiers along the highway.

Until recently, such technology was the privilege of a tiny section of Indians — engineers in the country's software hubs who earn more money while in their twenties than Bithoor farmers do in a lifetime. India churns out 300,000 engineers each year and is a growing software power, but farmers are the backbone of its economy. Infothela seeks to break the disparity that confines access to technology and growing affluence to the cities.

Many Indian villages are poorly wired – landline telephones can go dead for weeks at a time — making wireless technology the most reliable Web connection. The mobility of a cycle rickshaw, which is light enough to cross muddy, potholed roads, ensures that the same computer and Internet connection can be used by people in several neighboring villages. The Infothela cart has a specially designed frame and cushioning to protect the computer and accessories from the bumpy ride.

The mobile platform is necessary to reduce cost of ownership because the resources are shared by a larger population. It is also necessary to push information to women and elderly people who can't travel outside their village. The service is free for now, but fees will eventually be charged.

Rural women are learning computers. 'I want to see the world'. A few miles from Bithoor, another cycle rickshaw carries its high-tech load to Gorahah village, where men and women gather side-by-side for a class on electronic mail. The mix is nothing short of a revolution in tradition-bound rural India, where women are often kept indoors.

"We are now learning computers. There is no point if we can't use that new knowledge. We have to go out and do something worthwhile," said a woman who also attends college.

The classes teach the basics of computing, word processing, spreadsheets, Internet browsing and Web cameras. Once they learn how to use a webcam the villagers can take part in online classes, something the info-cart organizers hope to implement later.

The simple lessons are a big privilege in an Indian village, where half the population can't read or write.

In Bithoor, which is mired in tradition and poverty, Anju's parents plan to take her out of school in about three years, so she can be trained in domestic chores and married by 18. But a brush with computers has made her look beyond cooking and washing. "I want to work and make a name for myself. I want to see the world," she said, adding that she hopes to get a job in the city and then travel more widely. Anju said she has not disclosed her plans to her parents lest they stop her from attending computer classes, "But I know what I will do" (2006).

Information on various topics and sectors through computer learning can help rural women move from tradition and poverty and look beyond the village, household chores drudgery or just marriage at an early age. They can dream of seeing the world by travel and work which they see through TV images.

***Story* 3.** Benefiting rural communities through appropriate computer software, Centre for Development of Advanced Computing (C-DAC), Bangalore, ITC Research and Training Center in India, has developed two software applications catering to the needs of people in rural areas. The first, called Vyapar, is an online trading tool. The second, ECKO, provides a framework for building e-communities through collaboration and knowledge sharing. The software is being piloted with local organizations in India. ICTs can be used to assist small- and medium-sized enterprises to increase productivity, efficiency, and participation in the local and global economies.

***Story* 4.** As most of the women in Aruna's rural Gujarati neighborhoods are illiterate or semi-literate, video is a powerful teaching medium. So Aruna and her colleagues make videos around health and education themes covering everything from AIDS and literacy to assertiveness training. They use locations and people from their own community which enables the learners to relate more easily to the content.

"Initially villagers were very suspicious and we had to build up a rapport with the village chief but gradually we were trusted and now the rural women are actively using video to empower themselves."

Video SEWA is so competent that they were appointed by the state to document the Queen of Bhutan's recent visit to the region. "There we were among all the big shot press men of the world but we held our own and produced some excellent footage." One World South Asia has also commissioned Aruna's video group to document their conference events which is "yet another boost for our morale and great experience to help us improve."

***Story* 5.** Lakshmi is an ICT researcher at the Pondicherry branch of the M.S. Swaminathan Research Foundation (MSSRF). Specializing in rural women's agricultural network, Lakshmi is helping to develop an information village centre.

"We're linking up twelve rural villages across Pondicherry, providing them with computer and internet access so that they'll have more immediate information to help them in their farming work."

Through the Information Village Centre, the farmers can check weather forecasts, bus timetables, crop prices as well as get advice on best practices when it comes to buying seed and growing their produce. MSSRF is a centre for research on sustainable agriculture and rural development which has been in operation since the mid-eighties, bringing much needed insight and guidance to the grass roots rural communities in the region.

So what does Lakshmi and the other grass-roots women want? "Listen to our voices — we'll make 100 points and may be you'll hear at least one. We want to expand our services but we need more investment in the basic ICT infrastructures in our local Indian communities, most of which are very poor. Hear, what grass-roots organizations like ours have to say, then make an agenda to develop ICT infrastructures for us so that we can exchange and share knowledge."

Story 6. Wireless for the Women. "Where I come from, you need very strong muscles to walk the steep hilly paths," says Pratima, a tribal woman from a mountain village near Dehradun in the Northern state of Uttarakhand. "There are lots of wild animals but locals like me live with the animals as friends," she states. It's probably this fearless practicality which enabled Pratima to pioneer a wireless alert system in her mountain neighborhood where she works as a health and education coordinator.

There are no telephone or power lines in Pratima's community. "I'd visit women in the mountain villages in the morning but if there was an emergency later in the day when the men folk were at work, the women had no way of getting help. That's when I figured we needed some technology to link up these isolated communities."

The system is simple – walkie-talkies powered by batteries and operating from four nodal offices in the region. "Training is straight-forward. We tell the women about frequency and how to operate the system, switching it on and off, talking clearly into the speaker and most importantly of all, the need to share the responsibility for recharging the battery," says Pratima.

But that's a task in itself given that the spare battery can only be re-charged using power supplies down at the town market. So whenever a family is due to sell its produce, they take turns in bringing the battery back and forth for recharging. "It's worth the effort," says Pratima. "Now if a cow gets sick, a woman's about to give birth or there's a criminal element hanging round the villages, we can use the walkie-talkie to get help."

Story 7. After 14 years of campaigning for better health facilities in her Delhi neighborhood, Asha is now a respected mother figure in her community but it wasn't always like that.

"People were very suspicious at first. No one would listen even though facilities at our local dispensary were so bad that a pregnant woman would have to carry two buckets of water with her if she wanted the doctor to help her give birth."

Asha laughs now at how ludicrous the situation was but the reality forced her to act. "We live in an urban slum which is one of the poorest parts of Delhi. With no proper water supplies, people depended on tankers to come every three days but these tankers were very often unhygienic, never mind the containers that people used to collect the water. I knew I had to do something about it."

Even though health care was free at the local dispensary, Asha discovered that most people were unaware of this. "They might come once but if the doctor wasn't on duty, they'd never come back. I decided that we needed a telephone helpline where patients could phone to check surgery times as well as get health advice for common ailments."

The phone line was so successful, that with the support of One World South Asia, Asha campaigned to get a permanent supply of water into the dispensary. She continues to promote better health and education services for her urban community. She is thrilled to be in Geneva where she has the chance to learn from other groups about how they're using ICTs in their work and hopes to bring that back to her own people.

Story **8.** The Internet itself isn't creating new forms of crimes against women and children. But, it is sure generating powerful new ways and means for these crimes to be perpetrated. Women's movements have to deal with the issues of cyber-stalking, pornography on the Internet, SMS harassment, and what one research paper calls 'teledildonics'. Can the intersection point between ICTs and violence against women be redefined, or at least better understood?

These stories point that ICTs research can create new demands for new communication practices as well facilitate these practices. The developing countries can bridge their digital divide by looking for innovative practices in this context. 'ICT research and new communication practices' given in Appendix 1 is pointer to it.

Creating ICT platforms such as conferences, discussion forums could be catalysts for more pro-active ICT interventions in support of the work of the NGO sector, both from within and outside the sector. Although these initiatives are successful in their own right, closer alignment and engagement with other ICT stakeholders and initiatives could strengthen these efforts in encouraging NGOs to take a more active interest in ICT issues, sustain and expand this interest, and harness the power of ICTs in meeting their development goals.

Our discussions about the democracy of Information and Information flow, Communication Technology as facilitator, technology context for businesses and various innovative technology updates, civil society organizations, private and public sector ICT products and services providers, pro-active ICT interventions in NGO sector, ICT platforms such as conferences, discussion forums and Universities can contribute to global empowerment.

We expect enhanced global empowerment; when technology bridges the digital divide between developed and developing nations by interdependency loop; when technology, political and social Will bridge the digital divide between various segments of society — rural and urban, between higher and low socio-economic strata and between higher and lower educated. The later sets the stage for people empowerment which leads to enhanced global empowerment.

'The Technology Bridges' facilitate development and global empowerment.

Summary

Communication and information is power. Information flow and sharing of information is important and acquiring the relevant information empowers you to deal with the issues effectively. Democracy of communication is significant in this context. The bigger change now is that we are moving from a world of transactions to a world of interactions in a non-linear fashion.

We are experiencing change in communication practices — no censorship but regulations, right to information to its citizens, and information flow for people and businesses at home and abroad. These will create healthy growth of communication channels; and make issues transparent, accountable and participatory.

Technology has given promise for the effective progress of businesses. The lower cost, higher performance and advanced features of business technologies have benefited consumers. Therefore, technology not only has to keep pace with changing business requirements but also outstrip them by coming up with the next big revolutionary idea.

The next big thing is more about services, processes, business models or cultural innovation than just product innovation. Converging technologies, technology services led economy rather than technology products will be the driving force for growth of economy.

Technology companies worldwide are trying to bridge the digital divide among the rural and lower socio-economic population in developing countries through ambitious programs by multiplying the effects of computers, Internet and education to accelerate the reach of technology benefits. While the emerging markets, including India, present a significant business opportunity for these technology companies, it is also good to act as good global citizens. Their approach to emerging markets goes beyond simply providing low cost components. Instead, the companies believe people in developing nations require the education, Internet connectivity and the access to the right technology to meet their unique needs; where consumers must cope with a lower income and limited access to credit. These are the next steps for developing Information Society among the poor and rural population by bridging the *digital divide*. Overcoming the digital divide in conjunction with other socio-economic divides will remain one of the key development issues for decades to come.

The changing communication practice in India and elsewhere in other developing countries is to provide telephone connectivity as well increase tele-density in rural areas through cellular technology. It is cheaper and does not require rural electrification.

Cheaper cellular technology both hardware and software is creating wider and bigger markets even among the poor and bringing better connectivity and social change among the developing countries.

The key to unlocking ICTs for development involves a focus on a range of parameters which can be referred to as the 8 Cs of the digital economy: *connectivity, content, community, commerce, capacity, culture, capital and cooperation.*

The big question is whether Communication Technologies are facilitator or divider for the people and societies at large; and the world markets. We believe technologies are bridges for gap between existing and the innovations, gap between have and have-nots and 'The Technology Bridges' facilitate development and global empowerment.

PART – II

Enterprises, Markets: Globalization Contexts

4

Globalization of Enterprises, Markets: Emerging Practices

Size of a business alone does not spell success;

Networking is needed in the interdependent business ecosystems today.

Enterprises, Markets

We presume global empowerment is through Enterprises and Markets in different parts of the world separately and in conjunction with others, integrating and collaborating. This relates to capital, products and services, productivity and technology, human resources. Globalization is creating enterprises and markets of a different nature, through different demographics and in different geographies. Varied factors account for that. Among several other factors, we focus on Outsourcing and Advertising, Business competition and Business innovations as the major parameters contributing to global empowerment.

Part 1 discusses the globalization contexts of Enterprises and Markets and the upcoming Creating Enterprises through global Outsourcing and Advertising. Managing these Enterprises and Markets through Business competition and Business innovations in the global contexts is important and calls for decision-making in various contexts. Four chapters in Part 2 discuss the emerging and changed practices in these segments and to what extent they are facilitating global empowerment.

Management of business is about human beings. It is about making them capable of joint performance, to make their strengths effective and weaknesses irrelevant. Management deals with integration of people. It is deeply embedded in cultures. What they do may be the same. How they do it will be different. Every enterprise is a learning and teaching institution. Training and development must be built into it at all levels. It never stops. Profit is not the explanation, cause, or rationale of business behavior or business decisions but rather the test of their validity. True marketing starts with the customer, his demographics, his realities, needs, values. Business asks what the customer wants not what it wants to sell. Management, he once said, "deals with people, their values, their growth and development, social structure, the community and even with spiritual concerns" (Peter Drucker). *All these business management variables need communication strategies and practices. These practices change as these variables change to meet the demands of business and administration.*

Rajat Gupta, UN advisor to Adnan Kofi (2005) said, "I cannot envision an effective development strategy — uninformed by private sector." Government, society, businesses are interlinked in reaching development, empowerment and dignity goals. We operate as partisans. We fail to explore avenues of cooperation to work together. We fail to see the simple truth that there is no development without businesses and in the long term no hope for business without development.

We face three scenarios, viz. creating enterprises and markets in globalization contexts:

***Scenario* 1**

By comparison with previous periods, globalization today combines a remarkable confluence of dense patterns of global interconnectedness, alongside their unprecedented institutionalization through new global and regional infrastructures of control and communication, from the WTO (World Trade Organization) to APEC (Asia-Pacific Economic Cooperation). Driven by interrelated political, economic and technological changes, globalization is transforming societies and world order.

Contemporary patterns of globalization are associated with a multilayered system of governance, the diffusion of political power, a widening gap between the richest and poorest countries, and the further segmentation of societies into 'winners' and 'losers'. As a consequence, globalization has become increasingly politicized and contested. National and transnational social forces compete, within and outside prevailing structures of global and regional governance, to resist, promote, manage or direct its impulses. This is evident in, amongst other things, the contemporary debates about reforming global finance, ensuring universal human rights and regulating the trade in genetically modified crops and organisms.

"Contemporary patterns of globalization mark a new epoch in human affairs. Just as the industrial revolution and the expansion of the West in the nineteenth century defined a new age in world history so today the microchip and the satellite are icons of a new historical conjuncture."

Scenario 2

Sandwiched between the global forces and local demands, national governments are to reconsider their roles and functions. It is frequently alleged that the intensification of regional and global political relations has diminished the powers of National States. It is also sometimes asserted that the National States is as robust and integrated as it ever was. However, while regional and global interconnectedness are transforming State power and the nature of political community, any account of this as a simple loss or the diminution of national powers distorts what is happening as does any suggestion that nothing much has changed. *The States are powerful though the demands upon them have grown rapidly as well.*

Increasingly, the nurturing and enhancement of the public good requires coordinated multilateral action, e.g. to prevent global recession. At the same time, the resolution of trans-boundary issues may often impose significant domestic adjustments. In this respect, *politicians are witnessing a reconfiguration of State power and political authority.*

This is articulated most visibly in the shift from government to multilevel governance as States have become embedded within global and regional regimes. In essence, in a more complex transnational world, States deploy their sovereignty and autonomy as bargaining chips in negotiations involving coordination and collaboration across shifting transnational and international networks.

The power, authority and operations of national government are, accordingly, altering, but not all in one direction. The entitlement of States to rule within circumscribed territories is not on the edge of collapse, although the actual capacity of States to rule is changing its shape. A new regime of government and governance is emerging which is displacing traditional conceptions of State power as an indivisible, territorially exclusive form of public power. *Far from globalization leading to 'the end of the state', it is stimulating a range of government and governance strategies and, in some fundamental respects, a more activist state. There is transformation of State power.*

These developments pose very significant questions for democracy since the expanding scale on which political and economic power is exercised frequently escapes effective mechanisms of democratic control. Democracy remains rooted in a fixed and bounded territorial conception of political community. *Yet globalization disrupts this correspondence between national territory, sovereignty, political space and the democratic political community; it enables power to flow across, around and over territorial boundaries.*

Globalization therefore generates new political tasks, such as: i) Intellectual recasting establishing notions of social justice, equality, and liberty into a coherent political power to confront a world in which power is exercised on a transnational scale. This involves reconstructing the principles which underpin the democratic political community and citizenship for an epoch marked by transboundary politics and overlapping communities of fate. ii) Combining the institutions and practices of democracy with the effective governance of globalization within regional and global (public and private) authorities. *Globalization is not narrowing or foreclosing political options and discussion; on the contrary, it is re-illuminating and re-invigorating the contemporary political terrain.*

Scenario 3

People avail of opportunities to maximize wealth. While somebody finds an opportunity in IT services, another finds opportunity in weak controls in his organization to be exploited. It is the opportunistic behavior of individual which motivates him into action. Incentives and motivation created by organizations' controls and policy framework is important to optimally use these opportunities.

People, who have power, create systems which they perceive as good. Sometimes, large periods of neglect create abnormalities in system due to outdated procedures and rule framework. If the system is not responsive to the needs of the users of the system, the users, themselves not being able to change, adapt to the system and try to find loopholes which suit them. This is not a healthy situation. Participation in globalization will call for not only change in the outdated rules and procedures but creation of a new set to compete and adjust with the changing global realities whether in business, trade and economic growth and social growth. In short, change will be inevitable in attitude, behavior and thinking to achieve growth. This will call for demands on both people and governance.

Current globalization has provided opportunities to one and all, big and small, companies and individuals, national and local governments and the international community. What is more significant is that operational work areas and geographies are abundant and it has the technologies of global interconnectivity like Internet and telecommunications but there is worldwide competition to be the winner. What is more significant is that people themselves have to avail of these opportunities and turn them around for optimal gains. They are the losers in globalization race if they let the opportunities bypass them. Realizing opportunity cost will make them global winners or losers. This is equally true for nations and its governance, enterprises and its products and services for global markets and the individuals in various capacities.

All the above three scenarios call for different practices. Those practices are likely to undergo change also, as the global perspectives will be continuously changing. Equally significant will be how emerging concerns are communicated.

With globalization becoming the rule, the very business of business is changing. Varied business practices, increased competition and rapidly shifting consumer psychographics have given rise to the necessity of demanding new strategies, new mindsets, and new competencies amongst the business community.

The business practices will develop with focus on enterprise, market and learning domains. The enterprise domain looks at how we organize to create economic value and how we define the boundaries of these economic entities. The market domain explores how we compete and collaborate on a global scale to create, deliver and capture economic value. The learning domain seeks to describe how we learn, with particular emphasis on the interaction between individual learning and group learning to find new practices to create, deliver and capture economic value.

Companies are going from national to MNC and to globally integrated model. What is the difference between MNC and one having a globally integrated model?

In early part of this century, especially the war years, market access was important. Some global operations were multinational operations. The shift in today's world is that it's much less industrialized and much more service oriented. Globally, there is phenomenal intellectual capability and talent in the entire global community. The potential to tap that is huge. This leads to globally integrated model.

In the last two hundred years, globalization was driven by the differences between countries. There was one way flow of products, and goods were shipped from countries with abundance to countries of scarcity. More recently, the differences have led to some arbitrage. But to maximize the benefits of globalization, you have to take advantage of the similarities, and the differences too.

Companies with global ambitions should take advantage of globalization. Such companies may use highly efficient manufacturing base in China to produce low cost PC but also procure sales and support in Brazil, or get intellectual property from US or Japan. Companies can keep some functions with themselves and outsource functions which aren't its core competencies and leverage the IBM relationship for so many things globally.

Does globalization affect small and medium companies as well? Small companies may believe that globalization doesn't affect them, but they are affected the most. The market dynamics are very different today, and a lot of companies will have serious issues.

"IBM has a unique culture, and most executives in senior positions have lived abroad. 65% of our revenues are non-US, people are ready to work all over the globe. They find it a great experience. Some of our most creative work is done in a collaborative way. A great example is the cell processor. It was a collaborative effort of Toshiba, Sony and IBM. We are blessed with people who don't have a problem working away from home. In IBM, diverse groups engage in unique work, and it's our culture. We have been doing it for 100 years" (Sam Palmisano from IBM).

A demographic shift is happening globally, as resource reallocation happens worldwide, and that's affecting the flow of work. For instance, India has a huge young population; more than 50 per cent of Indians are less than 25. Western countries have been in a state of denial regarding the age factor, but they will have a large percentage of ageing population. Many of the young Indians will be needed to service these markets. Compelling demographics is also one reason why work will flow to India. This is part of the reason because of which globalization is coming to India. *Movement of people helps in the movement of skills and expertise from the developed countries to the developing countries.*

Globalization: Communication Practices

Communication practices in many domains are changing because of globalization, i.e. thinking globally. Let us reflect more on it and discuss how this is changing the practices, and its impact on them from various perspectives. As a fallout, the business practices are also changing around the world and the three key situations and trends that are significant in these contexts are: globulation, glocalization and globalism. It is equally important to understand the economic sociology and management strengths and lessons that impact the global businesses. The innovations get globalized because of democratization of information and technology.

The business model being followed is: open economy, liberalized economic policies, collaboration and interdependency, export oriented economic growth through export of products and services specifically produced for exports to developed countries; and import and transfer of technology, innovations and innovative business ideas from developed markets, expertise through foreign experts and expats. These kinds of exports and imports will create economic growth and steady the economy by producing more employment, circulation of money through foreign funding, more infrastructure and consumerism.

These are changing business communication practices in three ways. Firstly, i) people have access to varied businesses and new businesses associated with them, such as, cross-cultural training and culture and communication training programs. Call centers, BPOs and KPOs are new businesses associated with outsourcing. Offshoring of products and services may create new design centers, skill training programs and product quality controls measures in the host country. ii) The products produced in emerging markets for export to developed countries, as a fallout may create consumerism in the domestic markets and consumerism may be further promoted by higher disposable income of the younger generation. The higher disposable income is also the result of higher employment due to changing businesses and practices due to globulation, glocalization and globalism. iii) The emerging markets of India, China, Brazil and Russia and many other developing countries are participating in globulation by opening their economy, liberalizing economic policies, by allowing circulation of money by investing in foreign markets as well as allowing foreign investments in their countries. Thus businesses get expanded. Businesses get further expanded by acquisitions and mergers and by collaborating with foreign businesses to gain technology edge and markets and to expand in scale.

Secondly, foreign funding is invested in emerging markets in businesses in general, manufacturing of products and investments in stocks and bonds. Foreign investments create different kind of, and mutually facilitative opportunities for emerging markets, developing countries and developed countries.

Thirdly, technology changes how you do business these days. It is a great facilitator in many ways. i) there are quick travel modes, innovative telecommunication modes such as computers, cell phones, Internet functionalities, digitalization, data banks and data storage, and telephone, audio, video conferences etc. ii) Innovative business technologies shared by transfer and buying technologies, hiring expertise, business collaborations and creating innovations. iii) The sectors being focused currently are: in energy sector, petroleum and natural gas, fuel technology such as ethanol and glycol producing, wind and other power producing technologies. Mines and minerals are concentrating on steel, copper and calcified coal. Pharmaceuticals on drug research and development and marketing. Breweries are finding new ways to brew spirits from cereals rather than from molasses. iv) Technology of Internet has created e-commerce as a new mode of doing businesses; international market research, research and development and advanced analytics. v) Many Software programs, RFID and other barcode technologies have enhanced many business functions in many areas from banking, stocks, trading, retailing as well management of these businesses efficiently, in less time and with more global visibility.

Emerging business practices are changed practices in many areas though differently in many countries around the world. The trends are changing. Some of the significant areas of changing practices are: outsourcing, offshoring, advertising, competition in business, technology context, rural markets, microfinance, acquisitions and mergers, diversifications of businesses, enterprise architecture (EA), in restructuring plans of corporate, global banking , eco-sociology, foreign investments in stocks in emerging markets and business innovations, risk management of devastation and disaster management.

The practices related to inter-country related economy demands are changing such as focusing on China and India and what they can learn from each other and what MNC can learn from them and by doing businesses with other countries. The changing practices call for diversity in global economy and immigration management in global economy and many more areas.

Every business big or small, MNC or even individuals want to participate in the global race. The rush to be an achiever, to be the industry leader leads to competition and competition creates achievements and competitive edge. Competitions push for business innovations and new products and services for consumers which are shared not alone by specific countries but shared globally. Therefore, the impact of competition and business innovations is global as well as globally shared. Competition drives businesses to adopt new practices; as well competition pushes businesses to look for new and best practices to produce the products and services as well to deliver them to the consumers.

Market openness with globalization has increased the speed, frequency and magnitude of access to worldwide markets, including all tangible and intangible aspects of commerce, by a new and more diverse set of competitors. The motivations and drivers that engender fundamental changes in the industry structure include market factors, cost sensitivity, governmental influences, and competitive considerations. These factors have influenced the convergence of consumer expectations which, in turn, elicit responses to provide for these requirements.

With fast track changes in globalization, over a period of time, we do expect more of changing practices both in supplier capability and buyer preparation and management both in business domains and in communication modes and challenges of outsourcing such as occupational and professional, human resource development, political, economic and social.

The globalization forces engender companies to develop a new set of competencies that would enable the generation of good returns in the global market-place. A conceptual framework that underlines the importance of knowledge management competencies in creating global market advantage is needed. *The knowledge management competencies focus on knowledge development of global customer, competitor and supplier; and inter-functional coordination and value chain coordination.* The relationship between global market knowledge competencies and global market advantage is partially mediated by company's responsiveness. Global market advantage is positively associated with company's strategic and financial performance.

Global Emerging Practices

These emerging practices will shape global enterprises and markets. The global cooperation, collaboration, and competition models will further add on to give them more stability, visibility, productivity and prosperity. We cite few instances.

Mahindra & Mahindra India is penetrating a US market long dominated by venerable names like Deere & Co in US. Then it's time to take a look at how globalization has come full circle. A new breed of ambitious multinational is rising on the world scene, presenting both challenges and opportunities for established global players. These new contenders hail from seemingly unlikely places, developing nations, such as Brazil, China, India, Russia, and even Egypt and South Africa. They are shaking up entire industries, from farm equipment and refrigerators to aircraft and telecom services, and changing the rules of global competition. Emerging markets will make up 69 per cent of all new car sales by 2030, compared with 26 per cent now.

Unlike Japanese and Korean conglomerates, which benefited from protection and big profits at home before they took on the world; these are mostly companies that have prevailed in brutally competitive domestic markets, where local companies have to be in highly aggressive competitive situation with homegrown rivals and Western multinationals every day. As a result, these emerging champions make profits at price levels unheard of in the US or Europe. Indian generic drug makers, for example, often charge customers in their home market as little as 1 per cent to 2 per cent of what people pay in the USA. Cellular companies in North Africa, Brazil, and India offer phone service for pennies per minute. Yet these companies often thrive in such tough environments. Egyptian cellular operator Orascom boasts margins of 49 per cent and Mahindra's pretax profit rose 81 per cent last year.

Lenovo Group, the Chinese computer maker, made waves last year by buying IBM's $11 billion PC business. Indian software companies — Infosys, Tata Consultancy Services, and Wipro have revolutionized the $650 billion technology services industry; and Johannesburg brewer SABMiller PLC is challenging Anheuser-Busch Cos.' leadership right in the US. These companies are just the first wave.

Brazil's Embraer has surged past Canada's Bombardier as the world's No. 3 aircraft maker and is winning midsize-jet orders that otherwise would have gone to larger planes by Airbus and Boeing. Jetmaker Embraer's sleek EMB 190, which seats up to 118, has taken smaller commercial aircraft to a new level with a fuselage design that offers the legroom and overhead luggage space of much larger planes.

Western telecom equipment leaders have long looked down on China's Huawei Technologies Co. as a mere copier of their designs. But in 2005, Huawei snared $8 billion in new orders, including contracts from British Telecommunications PLC for its $19 billion program to transform Britain's telecom network. The deal "sent a chill through the rest of the telecom manufacturers," says analyst Michael Howard of Infonetics Research Inc. in Campbell, Calif.

Many more companies are using their bases in the developing world as springboards to build global empires, such as Mexican cement giant Cemex, Indian drug maker Ranbaxy, and Russia's Lukoil, which has hundreds of gas stations in New Jersey and

Pennsylvania. What is surprising is the amount of progress emerging-market companies have made in the last few years.

Boston Consulting Group in a recent study (2006) identified 100 emerging multinationals that appear positioned to "radically transform industries and markets around the world". What makes these upstarts global contenders? *Their key advantages are access to some of the world's most dynamic growth markets and immense pools of low-cost resources, be their production workers, engineers, land, petroleum, or iron ore. But there is much more than low cost. They are proving innovative and expertly run business, astutely absorbing global consumer trends and technologies and getting new products to market faster than their rivals.* Techtronic, for example, was the first to sell heavy-duty cordless tools powered by lightweight lithium ion batteries to Home Depot in US.

Ram Charan (2006) points that globalization and the Internet are ushering in this "seismic change" to the competitive landscape, because they can tap the same managerial talent, information, and capital as Western companies, "anyone from anywhere who sets his mind to it can really restructure an industry," Charan says. "Make no mistake; this now is a global game."

US corporations, of course, have weathered waves of new rivals before. The 1960s and '70s saw the rise of Western European industrial groups such as Unilever, Philips, Siemens, and Volkswagen. *Yet this new group of game-changing companies is different on many levels.* For starters, the new players are coming from many nations at once and deploying an array of strategies. They're also arriving from lands that, while growing fast, remain relatively poor. Germany and Japan were industrial powers before World War II and built on those strengths to re-emerge as global heavyweights.

By contrast, China and India have begun to emerge from extreme poverty only in recent decades. Per capita income in China is still just $1,300 a year. In India it's $620. That sounds like a huge handicap for companies from those nations: It implies low-income customers, meager capital, and hand-me-down technologies. It also means struggling with arcane regulations, corruption, and poor infrastructure. But by their business strategies, talent pool and getting into update technologies; they are changing the scenario fast.

Hardscrabble origins can be a vital source of strength. These companies have learned to make money by developing reliable, easy-to-use goods and services at very low prices. And those skills have equipped them well for operating elsewhere in the Third World. Telcos such as Orascom and India's Bharti Telecom, for example, earn high margins while selling cellular service in some nations for 2 cents or 3 cents a minute, while América Móvil pioneered the use of pay-as-you-go cellular service that allows the masses to pay as little as $4.50 for a prepaid card. Of 1.2 billion new cellular-phone subscribers worldwide by 2010, 86 per cent will be in developing nations, estimates Pyramid Research in Cambridge, Mass.

The late 1990s proved to be a time of key opportunity for these companies. In the wake of financial crises in Asia, Latin America, and Russia, many Western companies and banks pulled back from all but a few developing nations. Well-run local players bought assets from retreating Westerners on the cheap and doggedly pursued opportunities from Nigeria to Pakistan to Colombia. From 1995 to 2003, the World Bank estimates, corporate investment from one developing nation to another, more than tripled, to $47 billion annually. It probably has neared $60 billion since.

That leaves the new multinationals in a strong position. Over the next decade, the World Bank projects, developing nations' share of world gross domestic product is expected to grow from one-fifth to one-third. During the next two decades, predicts Goldman, Sachs & Co., China, India, Brazil, and Russia alone will add to their populations some 225 million consumers who earn at least $15,000 a year.

The established multinationals still hold big advantages over the upstarts. Citibank, General Electric, Honda, HSBC, Motorola, Nokia, and Philips are masters at using low-cost manufacturing, engineering, and managerial talent from Bangalore to São Paulo. Few developing-nation companies have such management agility.

In China, consumer-electronics makers such as Bird, Konka, and TCL have stumbled because of overcapacity at home and poorly managed acquisitions abroad. "Everyone sees Chinese enterprises as a threat, but in fact they face a lot of difficulties going global, because of poor management skills." China is fast realizing it and is making quick efforts to train its future managers in western management styles and skills.

The best emerging multinationals, though, have earned profit; have built global research and development networks, and boast world-class management. Other emerging players are using their access to deep pools of low-cost local engineers and experience gained in developing nations to close the gap with Western incumbents. Just three years ago in 2002, Huawei was known in the US mainly as the company that Cisco Systems Inc. caught copying its designs. But Huawei changed its business tactics, spent $558 million in R&D in 2004 and employs 7,000 engineers at its sprawling Shenzhen campus, is winning respect globally. In 2005, 57 per cent of its sales were outside China. It boasts a 15 per cent market share in Asia and 9 per cent in Latin America, cutting sharply into Cisco's lead in those regions. Huawei is the global leader in the rapidly growing equipment market for voice-over-Internet protocol service. Besides, undercutting Western rivals' prices by 20 per cent to 50 per cent, Huawei is adept at designing equipment appropriate for developing nations.

Ranbaxy India may rank just no.14 in the $28 billion US market for prescription generic drugs. But it is a leader in nations like Nigeria and Brazil. It has earned goodwill by being one of the biggest suppliers of $1-a-day generic AIDS treatments to Africa at cost, and hopes to have its own new malaria drug on the market by 2008. It has also acquired smaller generic drug makers in Belgium, Italy, and Romania.

When Ranbaxy first began to market its drugs in Europe, recalls CEO Singh, its sales staff was often kept waiting hours before skeptical purchasing managers would hear their pitch.

Now, Ranbaxy is a top supplier in much of Europe, and 80 per cent of its $1.2 billion in revenues comes from overseas. It has staff in 49 nations, plants in seven, and an R&D team of 1,100 at its 17-acre campus outside New Delhi.

Ranbaxy hopes this R&D base will enable it to spring into the top five in the US by 2012 and to No. 1 globally, passing Israel's Teva Pharmaceutical Industries Ltd. It has 58 generic medicines pending at US Food & Drug Administration approval, including a version of the anti-cholesterol drug Lipitor. Ranbaxy's pipeline is the second-biggest in the generic industry. "By learning to compete in this environment, we have gained strength in development and marketing that helps us around the world."

How can Western multinationals respond? The first step is to begin respecting the new competition. That is the attitude David C. Everitt, president of Deere's, is adopting toward Mahindra. Everitt concedes the Indian rival could someday pass Deere in global unit sales. Mahindra dominates the Indian market, which is bigger even than America's, and is especially strong in the small tractors that account for two-thirds of US sales. But Deere is also picking up its game by, among other things, boosting R&D in higher-end tractors for mega-farms in the US, Europe, and Brazil, and expanding its own production in India and elsewhere. "We are not afraid of competition," Everitt says. "It gets the juices going and helps us find ways to be better."

Another strategy is to refuse to yield ground either at home or abroad. Last year, Whirlpool Corp. agreed to pay a surprisingly high $2.8 billion to buy Maytag Corp. It wanted to keep Maytag out of the hands of China's Haier which had made a rival bid. Cisco, meanwhile, is keeping up the pressure in China, Huawei's home market. Cisco continues to win large orders from Chinese corporations, has plowed $650 million into Chinese tech startups, and has forged a tie up with local Huawei rival ZTE Corp.

There is always the strategy of joining the new challengers. Nortel Networks Ltd. and 3Com have formed telecom equipment and design ventures with Huawei. Navistar International Corp. in Warrenville, Ill., has a joint venture with Mahindra to build trucks and buses for export. "These companies can be opportunities if you can work with them."

No matter how the big US companies respond, gone is the era when they could afford to wait for an emerging market to ripen, and then count on their ability to roll over the unsophisticated local players. "If you don't participate in these markets, you not only miss opportunities but also are cut out of all the innovation that comes from competing there," says University of Michigan management strategist C.K. Prahalad. "Then you won't be able to withstand the pressure when these companies come and hit you here."

Infosys Company provides worldwide comprehensive end-to-end business solutions that leverage technology for its clients, including consulting, design, development, software re-engineering, maintenance, systems integration, package evaluation and implementation, and infrastructure management services. It has set up facilities in US as well China, keeping India as base, outsourcing technologies products and services from there, and research and development. Wipro provides IT services in India, as well as research and development services and software solutions to companies worldwide. The company also maintains a presence in the Indian market segments of consumer products and lighting

Delhi Metro Rail Corporation (DMRC) in India is seriously considering creation of a consultancy wing to cater to global clients. After Sri Lanka, Syria, Pakistan, Bangladesh, Indonesia and Ireland, Vietnam has shown interest in Delhi Metro's success story. Although talks are at initial stages, DMRC may be roped in for preparing the blueprint for a 12.5 km-long metro line in the capital city of Hanoi, sources said.

"If more countries want to use DMRC's expertise, we have to play a larger role at the global level." In fact, DMRC undertook preliminary studies both in Sri Lanka and Syria to build metro systems in Colombo and Damascus, respectively. The Colombo project, however, got shelved because of political reasons. Many Asian countries are turning to DMRC because of its expertise on low cost metro system. "Ours is the latest technology, yet, it's the cheapest. Many countries want to involve DMRC mainly because of its cost-effective techniques. We are familiar with the environment here, and also, good at working in high density areas where problems like acquisition of land often crop up," the official added (2006).

Whether one chooses to confront or collaborate, the new multinationals are set to change the rules in industry after industry.

Creating Enterprises

5

Emerging Practices

Global enterprises and markets are created through outsourcing and outsourcing itself calls for advertising of a different kind. Outsourcing is applications of an entirely new concept and strategies and practices in global business. Global business is its very basis. Global enterprises are created through outsourcing, and for outsourcing, they deal with outsourcing of products and services. Global enterprises use advertising concepts, modes and applications. Since global advertising deals with enterprises, people and nations, and products and services that have to be presented differently to a global audience. New advertising practices have emerged in these contexts. New business and communication practices are emerging for outsourcing and advertising.

Outsourcing

The outsourcing is through call centers, Business processing offices (BPO), Knowledge processing offices (KPO) from developed to developing countries because of their certain given strengths of low costs, software efficiency and knowledge, talents, etc., different countries are identified on those strengths for different kinds of outsourcing models to earn more markets and profitability. Outsourcing has been contributing significantly to economic growth of the emerging markets. Initially, outsourcing started in 90s. *The outsourcing has been changing trends in its focused areas — expanding to more and more areas, expanding modes of outsourcing, from offshore to RIM in 2000 decades*. These trends have changed outsourcing business models. More and more countries are encompassed in outsourcing net.

Both human and non-human skills are upgraded to meet the demands of outsourcing. This has contributed to the growth of global economy.

Outsourcing and offshore Business models are now open to new combinations of outsourcing, service providers, and off-shoring. The outcomes of such business models are: globalization, global delivery models, multi-country supplier and delivery models, hub-and-spoke model in globalization of services, captive centers model, small and medium enterprises using off-shoring. There are product development and design facilities off-shoring model. The 'Second wave' model for expertise-driven jobs and the reverse outsourcing model RIM – remote infrastructure management is the latest trend in outsourcing models.

Selective outsourcing and consolidations in business is leading to standardization in infrastructure outsourcing. Remote infrastructure outsourcing model (RIM) is the fastest growing segment of the infrastructure outsourcing pie. According to an Edelweiss IT report (2006), a large number of multi-billion contracts are coming up for renewal, and the client organizations are likely to segregate them into smaller deals. Infrastructure outsourcing will continue to grow as onshore, offshore mix model with an emphasis on global delivery systems and disaster recovery management.

Other business models associated with the above mentioned outsourcing and offshore business models in the outsourced country are also contributing significantly to its economy. There is iGen consumerism model, intercultural learning and training models including language facility, and etiquette and ways of handling situations both in business and social set-ups, business culture learning and training models of both outsourced and outsourcing companies in different countries. They are offshoots of outsourcing and creating business and business models of different kinds.

The developed countries are outsourcing their various business processes to developing countries because of cheaper costs and thus more profitability. The capabilities, which are outsourced offshore, have moved from IT-centric functions into business processes. The complexity of these capabilities continues to climb with functions such as patent research, drug research and development, legal services and equity research beginning to emerge as the high-end of offshore outsourcing. There are services such as data entry, technical support and financial analytics, which require vastly different skill sets, end up being lumped together and evaluated as "offshore business process services".

America's outsourcing to India is approaching a new frontier — outer space. India and US space agencies signed an agreement on 9th May 2006 in Banglore, India. Accordingly, the Indian agencies will fly two American lunar mapping instruments in India's unmanned mission to orbit the moon, scheduled for 2008. NASA is taking advantage of India's more immediate and lower cost plans as the possibility of sending American spacecraft to moon remains possibility in the distant future. The joint space venture is part of Bush administration's efforts to forge close strategic partnership with India.

Educated English-speaking younger age manpower, IT-centric trained personnel, low labor costs, growing infrastructure, suitability of time zones and willingness of business and the government to regulate, facilitate outsourcing to developing countries. Broad categories like people, skills and availability; business environment, and financial structure facilitate it further.

Apart from cyber security, other issues that are critical to growth of IT outsourcing are infrastructure and human resources. For example, India has depth and breadth of technologically skilled labor, available at a low cost; English language skills that facilitate communications with the developed English-speaking countries; an improving telecommunications infrastructure and extensive IT experience but it still lacks the quality infrastructure like China. Though India has realized this lacuna and is working at fast pace to achieve it with foreign funding and investments. As a policy matter, India was cautious when to open the foreign funding, and with what limits and consequences in these sectors.

Different developing countries have different outsourcing strengths such as India has more IT-centric, software development strengths. China has manufacturing strengths both in garments and hardware mechanical devices sectors. Stiff competition is growing among countries with high or low strengths as outsourcing product and services scope is widening.

However, while complexity is increasing, respective cost expectations are not shifting accordingly. Selling BPO services is becoming tougher and tougher as clients get more knowledgeable about outsourcing, and competition increases with an ever-growing number of players.

Increasing acceptance for offshoring is a foregone conclusion for multinational corporations that must keep pace with global competition, global supply and global delivery models. The role of offshore outsourcing will continue to grow in importance as offshoring moves to a corporate "must have" and as companies develop more sophisticated global delivery models across IT and multiple business processes. We also predict the emergence of multi-country supplier and delivery models that span the globe from India to China to central Europe. In the client market, US companies will no longer be the dominant buyers as western European firms create strong demand for offshore services. A longer list of contenders only reflects the rapidly spreading interest around the world in getting a piece of the BPO action. Offshoring will grow in size and complexity as clients leverage on early lessons.

While the amount of back-office work that is currently sent outside their national borders by Western, European and Japanese companies is still a tiny fraction of the total amount of such work that these companies outsource. Still it constitutes a substantial source of revenue and employment for recipient countries, as India has demonstrated.

The increasing complexity of processes being offshored will lead to more wholly owned offshore subsidiaries for BPO, often referred to as captive centers. Existing captive shared services centers will become targets for further efficiency and expansion. *It predicts that over 40 per cent of offshore initiatives will not yield anticipated savings, scale or risk diversification. The key reason for these disappointments will not be due to supplier capability but buyer preparation and management.*

In 2006 the expectation was that small-and-medium enterprises would finally be clients for offshoring as they weighed the benefits of offshoring due to budget pressures and a more accepting political environment for offshoring.

Outsourcing Business Models

The next big emerging phenomenon is a hub-and-spoke model in globalization of services. Singapore already has become a BPO offshoring hub whose spokes extend to India, China and the Philippines, and some day could reach out to Sri Lanka and Vietnam. Dubai has the potential to be a Singapore-like hub in the Middle East. It is stable, forward looking and technologically advanced. While the role of BPO hub by definition will be reserved to a chosen few locations, the spokes are likely to proliferate. It is as much about labor availability as it is about cost.

A 'second wave' seems to be coming in offshoring of business processes in which English language fluency will not be a decisive factor. These will be expertise-driven jobs, requiring mainly the ability to analyze and solve complex problems.

For example, these workers may be involved in bioinformatics, or risk analytics for insurance, or scenario management in sell-side equity research, and then, someone in the US can wrap the English language around their work.

Some businesses are offshoring product development and design facilities. The apprehension in this scenario is technology leak to local competitors. For companies that rely on cutting-edge innovation, protecting intellectual property is critical especially as local competitors are also going up the technology ladder.

There are political and economic ramifications from outsourcing and offshoring. The challenges of these are also undergoing change with both outsourcing and outsourced countries getting more knowledgeable, more demanding and more cost conscious on one hand; and on the other hand the newer trends coming up in outsourcing such as KPO (Knowledge processing office) and RIM (Remote infrastructure management).

KPO: "KPO requires moving away from simply executing standardized processes to carrying out processes that demand advanced analytical and technical skills as well as some decision making", says chief of Evalueserve. Some of the destinations from where KPO services are being provided are India, China, Russia, Canada, Israel and the Philippines. Some examples of services in the KPO domain are intellectual property research, R&D in pharmaceuticals and biotechnology, data mining, and a range of analytical services such as equity research and financial modeling.

Typical users of KPO services are market research and consulting firms, investment banks and financial services institutions, and corporate planning departments of large Fortune 500 companies. These services can also be easily used by small and medium sized enterprises due to project-based nature of the work.

RIM is long-distance monitoring of computer networks. The workers at outsourcing centers oversee computer systems for clients abroad. Remote infrastructure management includes security, operation management and network management for them. Security is about protecting company's network against virus and hacking attacks. Operation Management ensures adequate capacity of data and analyzes patterns of data usage. Network monitors overall network and reviewing performance.

This is India's latest frontier on outsourcing. This business could be worth billions of dollars as multinationals try to cut costs and Indian outsourcers tighten security check on corporate data they manage. According to Indian industry estimates (2006), market is still small, only $300 to 1 billion though growth is expected. Nasscom India estimates that the market size will grow 60 per cent as the foreign companies cut costs by shifting information-technology services abroad.

In 1990, US companies, IBM and Electronic Data Systems Corp. pioneered the practice of managing IT system remotely and they still dominate the field. But Indian companies are gaining grounds by pricing services 40 per cent cheaper. IBM is responding to these threats by beefing up its operations in India, and playing to its global strengths, it is competing more than just price.

So far Indian companies have been hired to do specific software projects, with specific chores on IT systems but have not managed the entire networks or production sites. The multinationals outsourcing this type through RIM will be concerned about the security of propriety information. To reassure potential clients, Indian outsourcers are taking certain steps: They have tightened security check on corporate data they manage. Indian law-enforcement agencies are being trained to detect data theft, and database of employees at software companies is being built for easier track if they commit crime. The data base will include person's biometric – finger-prints, date of birth, education, family background.

Rim units at Indian companies were set up since 2003 and the business is growing fast. HCL Technologies, Wipro Ltd., and Infosys Technologies Ltd. are growing fast with RIM; and more companies are likely to take up.

Even as Indian IT companies vie for a share in $80 billion plus outsourced infrastructure management market, some industry players see a change in the demand structure. Increasingly, large customers are employing diversified vendor strategies. Customers are looking for different vendors for different sub-segments in infrastructure management space-network management, server management, helpdesk, desktop management, etc. Different vendors may be strong in different areas. For example, some vendors are experts in the helpdesk support; but onsite desk side support requires a different type of skill and employee base. Customers are realizing this and splitting up their infrastructure pie among vendors who can do each piece best; although this means larger management overhead. HCL Technologies, for example, is looking at a co-sourcing approach which outsource specific task of infrastructure management. Co-sourcing also had the advantage of collaborative approach, where the client own technology, and retain higher degree of strategic control over its IT operations. This, in turn, would lead to smaller deals, shorter contract periods and greater collaboration among the players - similar to one that's happening in the broader IT services market, observers say.

Offshored and remote infrastructure management segment is growing fast and India is among the countries best placed to benefit from it. Quoting a Nasscom study, an HCL Technologies spokesperson said, "An estimated 40-60% of the overall RIM pie may be efficiently delivered through a global delivery model. The growth in RIM is being driven both by demand from customers, and by the ability of Indian companies to deliver these services."

International connectivity and bandwidth into India is now relatively easy to come by. Therefore, services like managing servers and even providing production support are delivered effectively over a global network. Most important, Indian offshore providers have proven themselves in the related areas of application development and maintenance.

A report from Deutsche Bank says, "Most infrastructure management work is done offshore by 'old India hands' — customers who have used the India offshore model and Indian vendors for many years and are comfortable with the model". Observers add that the dominance of Top Five IT players in IMS was also due to clients' preference to offshore 'end-to-end' infrastructure management services.

India's export-focused software services companies are eyeing outsourcing deals on their home turf as banks and government departments step up spending on technology to cut costs and improve their efficiency.

Challenges of outsourcing: There are occupational and professional, human resource development considerations, political & economic ramifications and social challenges.

The outsourced countries have to face the human development challenges because of the widening scope of outsourcing and increase in quantity of outsourcing that would need more skilled and trained manpower in specified areas. These countries must spend more resources on educating, training in focused vocational and professional areas, and ongoing upgrading of these skills and training in new skills to meet the demands of increased outsourcing as well as the new trends in outsourcing. These countries will have great apprehensions about loss of outsource business if trained manpower supply is not timely.

There are economic challenges and ramifications on two counts: because of ever growing competition from other emerging markets for getting outsourcing business share and lack of timely trained manpower supply. Both can result in employment and revenue loss and so economic growth. What is to be outsourced also would need political nod and policy considerations for economy and employment and protecting own people's capabilities and sensibilities.

The social challenges for outsourced countries are to handle the changing social norms and values and the consumerism among younger generations who are able to earn more at a fairly young age. Though such consumerism is creating markets and boosting economy of host countries.

The challenges are further undergoing change overtime with both outsourcing and outsourced countries getting more knowledgeable, more demanding and more cost conscious on one hand; and on the other hand the newer trends and business models are coming up in outsourcing. The challenge of stiff competition is growing up among countries with high or low strengths as outsourcing product and services scope is widening though different developing countries have different outsourcing strengths.

Global Advertising. It is about creating awareness, information and knowledge about products and services and persuading customer to buy it to bring business and profits. To reinforce customer brand loyalty, more and more visibility is offered for products and services. Trends in creating brand awareness are fine lines between ads and entertainment. As a result, these brands can be found in a host of new venues: the Web, live events, cellphones, and handheld PC. The major objectives of advertising change stances according to the contexts of markets and customers. Advertising dimensions may be easier to deal with domestic markets and customers since you are in-group. But in international markets, the context, nature, operations, channels, messages would be comparatively more complex; and even the expectations from advertisements for businesses will be complex.

Globalization contexts have changed the advertisement practices. The countries advertise not only their products and services for which they are seeking markets in the focused country, but also they emphasize comparative advantages of those products and services in other foreign markets where they do business and also in their own home country. In addition, to market the products and services they advertise, advertisers project and build the image of their country and governance, business culture and business opportunities and cost; and talents of its people through advertisements. How businesses project the later aspect through their advertisements will bring business from other countries which are the focus of their advertisements; and will bring future businesses from other destinations where those advertisements are likely to get circulated.

Thus, in this changed scenario, what is important is international advertising, global channels through which the messages are circulated and are visible; and the messages fitting the business culture as well cultural practices of both the countries involved in the business deal.

Businesses target commercial ads at consumer durable and non-durable goods, and industrial products and services to international businesses and clients; and ads for its talents and business opportunities for outsourcing. There are international social ads for developmental projects, products and services. Political ads pertain to political communications about the national and international issues by the national and international leaders and civil society. Ads pertaining to elections are important in political communication. Medical ads pertain to medical services, hospital etc., diseases, and medicines and innovations in medicines and its delivery system both in national and international contexts. Entertainment ads are for entertainment programs of dance, drama, music, movies, theater, cinema houses, and museums, book discussion clubs, weddings and social programs and entertainment in general both on national and global channels. Besides telling us about programs, these ads also project celebrities associated with entertainment programs. These ads in general project the diversity of products, services and expertise, the business practices and policies of different countries in globalization contexts. We observe that multidimensional advertisements, in domains of commerce political and governance, socials, entertainment, medical; and focusing on markets in domestic and international geographies are intertwined.

These different kinds of ads are for their specialized domains, but they do overlap and present multidimensional advertisements. These different kinds of advertisements are presented in a variety of ways. Many of the conventional ways are undergoing changes due to technology and business advancements, and changes in consumer behavior.

The trends and practices for advertising for global business have also changed overtime. There are varied media channels for global advertising. TV and Internet channels are most significant. Internet channel is getting more and more powerful as the access of the people increases to this channel. Over the years, TV has gained comparatively wider reach because of affordability and efforts to install community TV sets.

Global outdoor advertising reach is through international airports where such advertisements are displayed and global travelers get exposure to products, services and techniques of display. Indoor advertising or more aptly called within the country exposure to such global advertisements is when foreigners are visiting the countries for businesses, tourists and for other multi-functions. When people of different countries interact in groups, conferences, and one on one; they are the most significant and important emissaries for projecting and building the image of their country and governance, business culture and business opportunities and cost, and talents of its people for global awareness, information and knowledge. It is interpersonal as well as global interaction with advertisements.

International strategy for marketing advertising: One global message would ring in many markets. Nokia Corporation, the world's largest cell maker is going global with its advertising to create a stronger more unified identity in the tough cell-phone branding war. The corporate campaign carries the slogan, "1001 reasons to have a Nokia imaging phone," is rolling out across Europe, Africa, and Asia and soon in USA showing up in television, print and online ads. It aims to send one message in all countries where Nokia is sold, a strategy that departs from past approaches that used different images and messages in different countries.

The campaign bolsters a continuing debate among marketers: Should advertising be local or global. As companies and cell phones in particular battle each other for brand awareness, it is critical for consumers to get a consistent message wherever they travel. With online advertising and even TV ads being downloaded and shared over the Internet, ads are spreading faster and with less control.

Marketers are also pushing for global campaigning because, if done correctly, the leading advertising firm achieves economies of scale. It can spread production costs across markets and small markets benefits by having the same quality, slick and creative ads as richer and bigger areas. Yet a global strategy has some risks. One-size-fit-all approach could translate into bad business, if consumers misunderstand the nuances or cross-cultural differences.

To combat concerns of losing local flavor, Nokia is making tweaks for different cultures. The current campaign will employ actors from the region where the ad runs to reflect the look of the local population, though they will say the same lines. Local settings are also modified when showcasing the phones, such as using a marketplace in Italy or a bazzar in Middle East.

Nokia can now more easily advertise globally because most regions of the world use the same cellphone technology, allowing it to rollout the new products across the globe simultaneously. Until 2003, it would launch different products in different regions at different times, so it could not use a unified ad. However it did a one shot global ad for its N-gage games in 2003 because it sold the game console around the world (2004).

Marketing advertising in the emerging markets: American and European consumer goods companies have hit a wall in their home markets; competition is fierce and growth minimal. But as these companies enter the fast-growing emerging markets of Africa, Asia, and Latin America, they face an equally harsh reality. The time-honored techniques that have made them leaders in developed markets — expensive brand building, frequent product enhancements, and sophisticated marketing are ill suited to the vast, but price-sensitive, middle- and low-ends of emerging markets. A study of 23 product introductions in such regions illuminates the operational and organizational approaches most likely to succeed there. The brand name products will always capture their share of affluent consumers. But in the low-end of emerging markets, companies should take their cues from local competitors: keep local managers in place, adhere to local standards of quality, and maintain the autonomy and the cost-efficiency of local operations.

Certain basic principles of advertising planning apply to all media, including the Internet both for domestic and international advertising. One, *know your target segment*; who it is, why it would want to buy your product and how it would decide on your brand over competition. Two, *your product offer must be compelling*. No amount of marketing budget can sell a product that is bad or not needed. Three, your *advertising creative must be attractive*. Four, very little advertising spends result in instantaneous purchase. Most of the spend helps build the customer's knowledge about the product category, the brand and its superiority over competition — and hence purchase always lags behind the spend by a finite time. Message presentation through advertisements is for the success of products and services salability and persuasion appeals. The format, content, appeal of the message is important for comprehensibility and cultural relevance

Online advertising

Internet has begun to attract the attention of advertisers. Various researches indicate that people with access to the Internet around the world spend a considerable percentage of their total media consumption time on the Internet. It is thus natural that an increasing number of advertisers are keen to understand the why and how of Internet advertising, and learn planning and delivering online advertising campaigns.

This new advertising medium brings with it its own distinct advantages and set of rules for success. The Internet, as advertising medium, scores over the conventional media on two counts: in its ability to provide for interactive communication where the advertiser can establish a two-way communication with the consumer and in its ability to target communication to a specific target segment around any geographies. It is imperative, therefore, that an advertiser leverages these two advantages to the maximum extent possible. The element of interactivity in online communication is largely a domain for creative planning and execution. This medium will have wider reach of consumer segments, product and services demand, faster and comparatively less expensive.

The Internet advertising is exploding. Advertisers spend billions placing text ads next to search results. The ad agencies and search engines have to scale and streamline their operations to cope with the sheer growth in Internet advertising. In the process, a new category of work is emerging, the digital factory job. Behind the Internet ad offerings, thousands of human workers are working on data round the clock. Every time you search the Web, the work of such human workers is there; such as the editor, who would do cut and paste digital data, search marketing specialists to type phrases and drive ad traffic, book scanner to flip book pages for digital photos, operator to type put business cards and contact information, and data entry operators.

The Internet differs from conventional media because conventional media like press and TV are push and broadcast in nature. All consumers of a particular edition of newspaper or TV channel get exactly the same information. It is then left for each consumer to 'consume' only such information as she/he needs or finds relevant. Thus, the challenge for an advertiser is to choose such editions or channels where most consumers for that particular media vehicle are also target consumers for the advertiser's brand. The emphasis is, therefore, on reducing wastage.

The Internet, on the other hand, is pull and multicast in nature. Each consumer of a website can choose to visit (or not visit) a particular site, and thus the consumer pulls desired information. The cost of consuming multiple vehicles (sites) on the Internet is almost negligible compared to conventional media. Further, it is possible for a consumer to have a personalized view of a particular website, i.e. view only desired information in a desired layout. A classic example is a web-based e-mail service. A consumer views only her e-mails and arranged in a manner (ascending by date or new messages at top) that she chooses. The challenge, therefore, for the advertiser is to ensure that his communication is relevant and part of the information pulled by the consumer.

While planning for advertising on the Internet, planners create two levels of plan. One plan identifies the sites, particular sections within those sites (sports, entertainment, etc.) and particular position on pages (top banner, side button, etc.). This planning is governed by an understanding of the traffic pattern (e.g. youth, women, senior citizens, young professionals, etc.) that the site would attract, which is governed by the content type, quality, etc. This is pretty similar to the process that is followed while planning for conventional media. The product offer must be compelling. Also, advertising must be creative and attractive.

However, it is the planning at the second level that differentiates the Internet from other conventional media. Internet plans allow for real-time targeting of communication based on various parameters. These parameters are such that their value can be determined only in real time, i.e. as it happens. Some of the parameters that are used for targeting are geography of the visitor (country/city), time of visit (morning/afternoon/ late night), day-of-visit (Monday/weekend). *The ability to 'read' these parameters in real time and then deliver an appropriate communication is what makes the Internet a powerful advertising medium.*

Take a nationwide pizza delivery chain. It may use geography and time of day/ day of week targeting very effectively. To start with, advertisements may be delivered only on weekdays as a majority of Internet consumers connect using office infrastructure. Additionally, the highest number of impressions may be delivered during the 11:00 a.m. to 1:00 p.m. time band to catch the 'hungry-and-planning-for-lunch' consumer. The relevance of the communication may be greatly improved if different creative is delivered based on the city of the consumer, so that the base message could remain the same but the 'phone-number-to-call' could be that of the visitor's city.

Internet plans also enjoy the leverage of high levels of course correction that are unheard of in conventional media. Extending the pizza delivery chain example, a quick analysis after, say, the first week of activity may reveal that: visitors to a certain set of sites are not clicking on the banners. Visitors from city A, C and D seem uninterested in pizza as lunch. Visitors from other cities prefer pizza not only for lunch but also as an evening snack. These observations can trigger course correction for the original plan. Impressions delivered on the 'non-performing' sites and to visitors from city A, C and D are reallocated to increase the impressions delivered to visitors from other cities and increase the number of impressions delivered in the new time band of 4:30 p.m. to 6:00 p.m. Such regular course correction provides for 'better-bang-for-the-buck' Internet advertising plans.

Take another case. A leading portal in India aims at developing the 'learn-at-home' concept. There are two sets of target groups: IT-aware, i.e. training managers and IT-novices, i.e. students. The first level plan arrived at a list of websites that were frequented by the target segment. A total of 13 creatives were served in the first week. The main objective of the campaign was to enable a high CTR. Online planning and course correction led to a dramatic improvement in the CTR over the four-week period, up from 0.83 per cent to 1.63 per cent, an improvement of almost 100 per cent. Correlating various parameters like creative, site content, time band, city, etc., achieved this.

Surveys ads on Internet are changing the practice of how surveys were done earlier through other media polls. Survey ads may relate to any domain such as politics, social, consumers, commerce and businesses. These surveys have wider audience reach, more differentiated opinions and results are available quickly for action.

New strategies for engaging customers on the Internet are: i) Rally communities to build your brand. Customers can be your best persuaders, so do not limit yourself to broadcasting messages from the media only. ii) Tap the wisdom of the crowd. Viewers, listeners, and readers are smarter than your employees. So let them improve your products and services. iii) Hire the ad geek. Do not try to guess which search words will bring in the most buyers; instead, bring in the experts such as search engine optimization firms. iv) Explode your brand. Forget about creating loyalty to a network. Viewers, readers and customers today care only about a particular show, but then they want to immerse themselves in it.

Participants in Brand Works University 2006 conference in Madison suggest that companies and marketers can create "brand fanatics" by recognizing the power of "online" and bringing consumers into their advertisements. Another suggested, using their brand advertising to drive Internet exposure and to engage customers in brand building. Another noted that there is still a huge gap between the amount of time people spend online and the amount of advertising dollars being spent online. Internet growth far exceeds any other medium, yet "a lot of folks don't fully understand the power of online creativity," she stated.

Among the best practices that facilitate online creativity are target marketing (for greater effectiveness), streaming video (stimulates interaction), and the combined use of display ads and sponsored search, or "meshing media". Everyone has a favorite television show where brand marketing can be used to reach targeted consumers and then drive online search, and more people watch their favorite TV shows with a laptop (and therefore the Internet) within easy reach. Getting your most avid fans involved in creating content and brand message is a triumph of experimentation with "cool, new things", "Take a bit of your (advertising) budget just to be experimenting on ways to connect with consumers".

Internet Advertising for Global Reach

Web is an effective and important advertising medium, *Web globalization is driven by a global economy, emerging markets, and a stronger appreciation for the value of multilingual Web-sites.* In addition, Internet users who do not speak English now outnumber the Internet users who do speak English. Multilingual Web sites are available to some extent. Companies in search of growth are looking outside of the US to emerging markets such as China, Brazil and Eastern Europe. They aim to reach people actively seeking information on their products and services instantaneously and interactively. The key is to create a Web experience that meets the needs of this growing customer base.

In today's online world, search engines have become the go-to resource for finding information about products and services. Having a presence on search engines for the terms relevant to the products or services, you provide a necessity for growing your business. Search engines such as Google and Yahoo are much in demand for their wider reach through specific country reach. Google and Yahoo's global reach and local language content offerings across geographic, demographic, and shared-interest and personalized properties, locally and internationally, provide unique and efficient advertising solutions that address a variety of markets around the world and help companies achieve a substantial presence on the Internet. Internet advertising provides customers with end-to-end global solutions.

The Internet (advertising) holds great potential as commerce and communication medium for companies and their customers, that they should make it an important and growing component of their worldwide media plan. Companies are making full use of Internet advertising by tailoring their messages to the different geographic, demographic, and shared-interest audiences which are delivered around the world. Even companies take an innovative approach by targeting individuals in several languages to reach all of its key audiences with personalized pages on search engines or sites to reach key demographic and international groups. For example, the IBM program/s has exclusive positioning in multiple directory pages, content areas, keyword search results, and specific audience packages at Yahoo site. Yahoo! provides similar global advertising solutions in a variety of categories such as automotive, consumer products, and entertainment, for companies interested in creating a significant presence on the Web across a range of targeted Internet audiences. Google AdWords ads connect you with new customers at the precise moment when they're looking for your products or services.

With the capability to target audiences globally through a single, branded, comprehensive source, the network of these websites offers advertisers a unique solution. The service provides advertisers with a growing audience of users internationally.

Moreover, some of the search engines, such as Google Personalized Campaign Creation by their Jumpstart specialists and Google AdSense, are a fast and easy way for website publishers of all sizes to display relevant Google ads on their website's content pages. The ads are related to what their visitors are looking for on their site—or matched to the characteristics and interests of the visitors their content attracts. Google keeps the users coming back with contextually targeted ads. It revs the site's revenue potential.

The ad sites such as Google does safeguard your business standards through certain filters such as Competitive Ad filters, i.e. you can block competitive ads, or other ads you want to keep off your site. Ad Review filter review ads before they appear on your site, they're reviewed using a combination of human and automated processes. The review process takes into account a variety of factors, including the quality of the ad and whether it is suitable for all audiences. At times, certain ads may be inappropriate for some pages. For example, Google automatically filters out ads that would be inappropriate on a news page about a catastrophic event through Sensitive Content filters.

Google has also attempted to create a network effect in its advertising business with its Google AdSense service. Google AdSense places ads on many small sites, such as blogs, using Google technology to determine which ads are relevant to which blogs. Thus, the service aims to serve as an exchange (or ad network) for matching many advertisers with many small sites (such as blogs). In general, the more blogs, Google AdSense can reach, the more advertisers it will attract, making it the most attractive option for more blogs, and so on, making the network more valuable for all participants. Google also advertises on its search engines the matching advertisements with the information that consumers want. It also localizes its ads according to the country and that make them relevant for marketing.

Global online marketing, multilingual Web promotion and website translation will develop international sales for the companies. It's like having your own international online marketing office in every corner around the world. The company can be on the map in each country market through expert online marketing work and targeted sales strategies designed for overseas marketing. Techniques such as index registrations, search engine optimization of home pages for foreign keywords, online promotion, strategic linking, and paid search engine advertising are all excellent in order to build traffic to target markets.

Internet advertising and global marketing for international audience demand extra attention. One of the keys to success is to focus on the targeted audience's frame of reference. You will need to step out of your own frame of reference and focus on making these salient for your target group.

Advertising on the cellphones

This is the next trend. In 2004, the standard web page banner ad is reformatted for a tiny cellphone screen. This is the latest foray in marketing. This could be an enormous new advertising market. Marketers can reach millions of people with personalized interactive advertisements whose effectiveness can be instantly measured by how many people click on them. Important bonus for advertisers is they have a consumer's number for future text messages. They are convinced about the potentialities of wireless marketing. The camera cellphone also opens up new advertising potentialities. The cost of producing cellphone ads is minimal. Marketers are feeling their way through issues like people's level of tolerance for screen clutter and their privacy issues. But consumers feel it would be invasion of privacy and they are concerned about privacy issues and scams like telemarketing.

Advertising on cellphones is the new communication practice. Advertisers are searching for right business model for ads on mobile. Several European companies sought ways to use the cellphone as a direct marketing tool around 2000. The device seemed ideal—it was highly targetable, it was interactive, and its small size and immediacy allowed quick response to changes in market conditions. But the privacy issue of the consumers could be of concern and block the ads.

A few factors are driving the interest in ads on cellphones. Increasingly, cellphones are becoming more data oriented and PC-like. The major factor is people are carrying it most of the time on their person though people may not be lugging laptop or TV with them. Comparatively, it is more accessible for ads. Consequently, there is now space that advertiser can use for marketing. The limitations of the mobile screen and the available bandwidth make full-blown Internet surfing a bit slow, so publishers have limited their content to news scrolls, sports scores, stock quotes, weather updates, and short video clips. Because of bandwidth and graphics limitations, the current advertising is limited to banner ads that offer the mobile phone user offers such as discounts or sweepstakes entries. The system provides what the ad industry calls a "call-to-action," in which the user must click on the ad or click to call some phone number to complete the process.

TSM (Three Screen Mobile) company has also been testing the possibilities for brand campaigns on mobile phones. Branding goes beyond product advertising by attempting to establish a company name or an image of that company in the consumer's mind. Generally, branding has been most successful on TV where the picture and sound technologies are richer than on the web or on cell phones.

Company can offer very precise demographic marketing. When the user clicks on an ad or keys in his or her city for weather information, he or she is providing valuable location information. That can be used to determine what ads the user should see.

In addition, cellphones are quite popular among a prime advertising demographic, i.e. youth, including college and high school students. The 'youth market' tends to be quite interested in products with short life cycles, such as music and movies. These products generate a lot of advertising because companies need to quickly create a buzz as new products arrive. While it can create interest in a product, it can also generate a negative message. Pop-up advertisements represent one area where companies found the medium hurt rather than helped brands. Vendors are moving cautiously, because little is known about the impact of cellphone advertising. To date, the market is more tailored, advertising to the mobile consumer is good for the customers and good for the brands trying to reach them. The advertisers can create compelling and entertaining ways to reach their customers, while keeping a great consumer experience at the forefront. TSM is also looking at bringing ads to mobile games and streaming video as both of those technologies are emerging.

Initially ads may consist entirely of repurposed TV spots; eventually advertisers will begin creating "made for mobile" ads once the market matures. But keeping in mind the limitations of phones' 2-inch screen, and targeting ads toward a younger demographic.

The market for video ads on cellphones is very small; MobiTV company is off to an early lead in 2005-6. Advertisers are testing out a variety of format on cellphones, including sweepstakes, voting, SMS campaigns, banner ads, TV ads on video, product placement in video games, and ring tone jingles. No one is really sharing statistics, but marketers are happy with most of their endeavors/experiments so far. We will see ad-supported video going forward.

Yahoo! is adding text ads that appear when people use its search engine from their handsets in Japan, and the company is auctioning spots on its mobile travel website in Britain. The trials mark Yahoo's first experiments with search advertising on phones and may provide an avenue to sell more ads to companies seeking to reach younger consumers. The company is competing with Google Inc. and Microsoft Corp.'s MSN for products that let cellphone users find restaurant locations, movie show times and stock quotes.

French-based multinational advertising delivery experts JC Decaux is about to unleash an interesting advertising scheme based on sending highly targeted ads to your cellphone as you walk by a billboard or a bus-stop. An initial trial will happen in France first, with plans already in place to expand the reach considerably. The idea has some potential, and something like this may soon be inevitable, but there are a few problems with it too, such as invasion of privacy.

Early experiments with JC Decaux' technology have involved finding a strategically placed ad transmitter box (about the size of a shoebox, and easily placed inside billboards or those advertising panels you see at bus stops), keying in an access code on the front panel, and then getting some sort of marketing message sent to your cellphone. When the real service rolls out, anyone who wishes to participate needs to register through a webpage, set up a profile of likes, dislikes, and what kind of advertising they want to see, and link that to their mobile phone number. It's an opt-in scheme, so if you don't want it, don't know about it, or just don't care, your phone won't receive any of these messages (2006).

Advertisers use tracking people technology on mobile phones. Why would your customers and potential customers agree to be tracked? Because by knowing where they are, you might be able to offer products or services they can't refuse. If you're a real estate broker, you could send an alert to the cellphones of house-hunters who happen to be within a mile of on-the-market homes that meet their criteria. If you're an insurance agent, you could let clients know their driving patterns qualify them for a discount. If you're in retail or hospitality, you could send out offers of discounts to the cellphones of passersby. "The game changes when you don't have to wonder where they are and what they're doing."

Earn free cell calls by watching video ads on the cell. Virgin Mobile USA, a cellphone service used mostly by teenagers and 20-somethings, said it was giving its customers the option to earn free calls if they view and respond to ads on their phones. Interesting offer for customers of Virgin Mobile, they can get up to 75 minutes of free calls per month if they spend an equal amount of time looking at ads and replying to these ads via text messages. Virgin, one of the first providers to offer such a service, hopes the service will appeal to its often cash-strapped customers, 65 per cent of whom are younger than 30 years old. Its first advertising partners are Pepsi, Microsoft's Xbox game console unit and Truth — a youth smoking prevention campaign. Advertisers see a "dual-revenue system" on the horizon, in which they'll sell music and other content to customers through ads.

Bar-code technology links with Internet, cellphone. Companies are seeking to make the bar-code technology easier to use by pre-loading it on mobile devices. Consumers, who are turning to their phones for a multitude of functions from downloading ring tones to text messaging to mobile web browsing, also appear more ready for the services, which are free excluding data fees. A rising number of people are using new free services to connect to the mobile Internet by photographing bar codes. The codes – either conventional bar codes or digital ones are showing up on more products, advertisements, books and even buildings. They are arousing the interest of advertisers who see the potential to serve up more relevant ads. For instance, a trailer downloaded off a movie billboard. Consumer-product companies are trying to make products more interactive.

Wireless Search Ads: Google signed a deal in May 2006 with the Japanese phone company KDDI to put its search engine into KDDI's EZ Web Internet service for its "au" mobile phones. It is also in talks with China Mobile about introducing a similar service in China. Google has been expanding its presence in the Asian market, introducing a Chinese version of its search engine, Google.cn, and buying a stake in Baidu.com. It also faces competition in Asia from its rival Yahoo which already enjoys a strong presence in Japan, as well as having many users in China. Both companies have run into controversy from their dealings with the Chinese government, however. The KDDI service is available since July 2006. It will combine search results for content aimed at both mobile phones and PCs. KDDI said it will also provide users with more direct access to information.

Tokyo-based KDDI also plans to take advantage of Google's vaunted advertising skills. Text ads based on search terms will appear alongside related search results. "Advertisers can apply for mobile AdWords", The two companies intend to refine the mobile search features going forward. In September 2005, Yahoo was reported to have begun testing the display of ads with Internet search results on cell phones in Japan. That may have helped encourage Google to make a deal with KDDI.

Advertisers increasingly are expressing interest in mobile phones because so many people have them. That, in turn, has led to a surge of interest in providing content to which advertising can be attached. Recently, for instance, a start-up announced that it wants to provide ad-supported comic strips to cellphones.

Companies are building databases of mobile-phone numbers so they can send text-message ads, but spam looms as a serious threat. With competition among the wireless carriers for supremacy, the real winner will not be decided by how many ads they can put out, but rather how many cellphones they can put in people's hands.

Weblog

Weblog is another practice in Internet communications. The blogging scenarios have changed in 2005. It is accepted widely as a significant mass medium with wider implications for personal and businesses, for individuals and groups, for governments and corporate. Its format along with its image is changing fast. This is now being considered as citizens' journalism and their views through blogging are accepted.

The latest in biogging is weblog search engine since it is not easy to find the latest today's buzz among the approximately 12 millions weblogs.

Tech-savvy bloggers soon figured ways to add audio-visual input into their blogs, so they weren't just text. Video blogs is another dimension of weblog communications on Internet. It started in 2004. Video blogs are pre-existing text blogs which include commentary and views on current events. These are amateur videos given on the blog. For example, Video blogs communicated powerfully about the humanity devastated by tsunami. The commercial future is emerging of online video distribution, using Vlogs to sell ads, and corporate sites to reach out to customers and suppliers.

But now due to blog craze and proliferation of high-speed broadband new pioneers are emerging. The development is due to spread of better distribution technology such as wider connectivity by broadband and adoption of blogging software such as syndication or RSS which let people customize content. With RSS people can choose the types of video they want to see and have it sent automatically to their PCs.

Companies are coming up for providing online storage and blogging room for creative types. Yahoo has launched a search service that uses RSS tools developed with *ourmedia* and *indie* site. There is site *Atomfils* to collect video from around the web. Blogs that sell ads are adding video product reviews.

Another Vblogging phenomenon is facilitated by pictures taken through cellphones. At places where people are not allowed to take cameras, people use cellphones with cameras to take pictures. If they choose, they can put these Vlogs of the events. In some of the recent terrorist attacks cell Vlogs gave the first hand and first glimpses of the attacks. These were of immense help.

Corporate blogging: Corporations have started setting up their own blogging sites as advertising channels. It is being used as an advertising channel versus traditional TV advertisements. They use it to get critical appraisals about their products and services from the public as well as feedback from the customers. It is a kind of unstructured research tool that they use. They do find the comments candid. This kind of advertisements and research, critical appraisals were not paid or solicited earlier but now the practice is changing. Corporations are sponsoring them. Some companies are hiring bloggers to project their products and services and setting up their own blogging sites as advertising channels. Not only this is much cheaper than the traditional advertisements or research projections; but it reaches a wider global public since Internet is clicked by millions all over the world.

Global Advertising on Conventional Channels

Conventional advertising channels through new and modified ad techniques are also being used for international advertising and marketing of products and services. TV is one of the major channels to project to the international audience as well the home audience at the same time. The limitations of TV advertisements are: i) There is audience fragmentation because of many TV channels, further threatened by electronic ad-skipping devices such as TiVo (video on demand on TV). ii) Ad clutter: The shortening of the product life cycles and emergence of new products in shorter spans of time has resulted in cluttering of products and competition for targeted customers. iii) The bombarding of the customer with frequent and boisterous campaign results in customer fatigue and burnout.

Customer's entertainment space hence gets jammed with these promotions resulting in customer aversion for newer brands resulting in lesser effective even the most creative advertisements. Companies must look into strategies of de-congesting the customer's entertainment space and elongating brand life time and product life time and allowing more time for customer to stay in each of the selection processes without having him hurrying through these processes adding more value to the customer with appropriate selection and higher value to the company with more satisfied customers.

New or modified ad techniques even on conventional media are being used for brand visibility: Some of these variations in Advertising situations are; dubbing product placements, changing ad pitches, international marketing with modified local pitches, guerrilla marketing techniques, addressable cable technologies, sensitizing employees to company's brands, marketing techniques applied to traditional media like films, and viral marketing through e-mails etc., direct-to-consumer advertising, opt-in-option, directing ads to segmented markets such as seniors, youth, rural markets and low-end consumers, comparative advertisements, people marketing techniques, and mystery shoppers.

Dubbing product placements. For decades film studios have been dubbing the dialogues. Digital technology has made it easy and inexpensive to substitute one product plug for another in the domestic and overseas version of the same movie. This gives studio revenue when they can sell product placement rights overseas.

Major studios set up units to sell roles, sometimes directly to advertisers, sometimes through agencies that concoct related promotions for the advertisers such as movie themed contests or store displays. With foreign markets contributing as much as 60 per cent of the box-office take for most Hollywood pictures, the practice of tailoring product placements for international markets is taking off. In some cases, the dubbed plugs are mainstay of a movie's global marketing campaign.

Changing Ad pitches: The marketers are learning that reaching consumers through advertising through traditional means —TV, films, magazines, newspapers is getting harder in the coming years. Consumers are seeking information from broader range of sources and filtering out messages that do not resonate or speak to their specific needs. Ad industry needs to reinvent itself and change ad pitches for new international targeted audiences.

Ad pitch for the wireless audience: Such things as blackberry, ipod and cellphone are intimate techy devices that have the potential to catch on-the-go consumer at the perfect moment to take buying decision. The cellphones are being used by teens for picture sharing and text messaging. As the mobile phone becomes more of a multi-tasker — to surf the web, watch TV and get text information; the distinction between various media platform is blurring. Marketers used to allocate separate budgets to print, television and the Internet but now they have to think differently. They may also seek marketing deals with controllers of electronic devices and designers of software that help consumers organize electronic media and entertainment choices.

Another hot area in advertising is *addressable cable technology*. It can deliver messages tailored to specific zip codes and neighborhoods. Advertisers can monitor through cable set boxes, the habit of watching on-demand movies and the potential for consumers to skip commercials. They can track who is zapping ads and perhaps figure out ways to get them to stop. Media buyers believe, the set-top boxes have the potential to give more exact audience measurements than consumer panels and sample groups. The marketers are seeking this new way to gather data on the audience for their promotions than to rely on the old fashioned metrics such as newspaper circulation and TV ratings.

Marketers have to use different techniques to reach the audience. The audience is getting more fragmented due to various media options. Marketers need to reach to consumers in individual situations, with ads that are tailored for particular individuals and not the world at large. Mass marketing is not going away but one-on-one marketing is becoming necessary. The key to 'getting to know you' technique with the audience is gathering personal information, which raises questions about privacy.

Direct-to-consumer advertising: Direct to consumer ads of Celebrex medicine are now embedded in entertainment programs. This kind of advertising for drugs is still in its relative infancy but consumers are chaffing at ads featuring cartoon characters, rhymes and jingles to sell medicine as if it were pizza. Pharmaceutical manufacturers may shy away from aggressive TV ads on these medicines and explore more low-key pitches and pursue subtler approaches such as possible opportunities in movies and TV shows.

Then there is *opt-in-option* where marketing maneuvers engage rather than intrude on the consumers. They make efforts to get consumers to expend energy by engaging them before they get a sales pitch. There are 'invitational' commercials that ask consumers to click to a particular website, send a text message, or e-mail, offer an opinion or follow up in some other manner that prompts involvement. These moves can be tracked and information they provide can be filed away for future reference.

Another new practice is to address the ad pitch to the aging population: Its new market is growing due to longevity; senior citizens have money to spend so why not target them for other consumer goods? Earlier, most advertisers were ignoring senior citizens. Many of them assume the ads targeted to young will also be seen by the seniors. Others take seniors for granted. Senior citizen market is a big market to be targeted both for products and services and need not be bypassed. Health clubs and fitness centers gear marketing to younger but statistics show that most of their members are 50 plus and they are regular and loyal. So should they not target the seniors in their ads?

Rural markets and low-end consumers: These need specific ad pitch not only for the products and services relevant to them but making them affordable also. Therefore, in these markets, both needs and affordability have to be focused.

Comparative advertisement: When it comes to marketing products and services, comparative advertising is happily tolerated, even enjoyed, by audiences—just so long as it is dished up with a healthy dose of humor. In addition, the claims must be true and documented.

Another type of subtle comparative advertisement is product-placement in the ads. The products are placed in the characters of the show. It is shown being used by them, such as a particular brand of car, furniture, etc. It is great for marketers when people do not pay much attention to traditional TV ads. TV networks and advertisers are finding that product-placement campaigns need to be constantly reinvented and keep coming with new ideas.

The negative ads are also comparative ads to create negative feelings for the comparative products. While attack ads cause audiences to experience negative feelings about the company being attacked, negative impressions also go up for the attacker. So while a two-company fight launched by the underdog may prove successful, if there are multiple companies vying for dominance, launching a negative campaign could give lesser competitors an advantage and the opportunity to leap ahead. If you're the market leader, launching attack ads may actually give your lesser-known opponent name recognition.

The various techniques of advertising through people marketing are being used: Companies co-create brands with consumers. Consumers subcultures are invited to help shape a brand's ideology, use, and persona. Even blogs are being used these days.

The practice of using Mystery shoppers as tool to evaluate all touch-points between the company and its customers is now being widely used by businesses to instill a sense of competition among dealers, to stimulate employees for better customer services for bonus incentives and over and above the companies get reality check assessment for their products and services and competitors fast and at reasonable cost.

Summary

Global enterprises and markets are created through outsourcing and outsourcing itself calls for advertising of a different kind. Outsourcing is application of an entirely new concept and strategies and practices in global business.

Outsourcing business models are changing over time from BPO, KPOs to RIM. Outsourcing creates occupational and professional, human resource development, political, economic and social challenges. These challenges get more demanding as both outsourcing and outsourced countries are getting more knowledgeable, more demanding and more cost conscious on one hand; and on the other hand the newer trends are coming up in outsourcing.

Different developing countries have different outsourcing strengths. Stiff competition is growing up among countries with high or low strengths as outsourcing product and services scope is widening.

Offshoring will grow in size and complexity as clients leverage on early lessons. A 'second wave' seems to be coming in offshoring of business processes in which English language fluency will not be a decisive factor. These will be expertise-driven jobs, requiring mainly the ability to analyze and solve complex problems. For example, these workers may be involved in bioinformatics, or risk analytics for insurance, or scenario management in sell-side equity research, and then, someone in the US can wrap the English language around their work.

Outsourcing constitutes a substantial source of revenue and employment for recipient countries, as India has demonstrated.

Global Advertising is about creating awareness, information and knowledge about products and services for the global audience through different channels such as Internet, cellphone, Web search engines and Blogs and also through conventional media channels. It is also about image building of the host country and the targeted markets. Outsourcing itself calls for advertising of a different kind. In international markets, the context, nature, operations, channels, messages would be comparatively more complex; and even the expectations from advertisements for businesses will be complex. Web globalization is driven by a global economy, emerging markets, and a stronger appreciation for the value of multilingual websites.

Managing Enterprises, Markets: Emerging Practices

6

Business Competition

Competition is imposed on us by a world
That has shrunk to a global market.

Enterprises and markets in the global contexts are managed through business competition and business innovations. These contribute to global empowerment. Many changed and new business practices have emerged when there is competition to go ahead. In this competition, they look for best practices and their functionality and success, learning from businesses around the world who have adopted them. Bartlett and Ghoshal (1999) point, a company's heritage can have a major impact on how it adapts to the new environment and that is often overlooked in the move into the international arena. In the book *Managing Across Borders: The Transnational Solution* they examine one aspect of that heritage: the influence on a company of its nation's history, infrastructure and culture. The influence of a nation's history, infrastructure, and culture permeates all aspects of life within the country, including the norms, values, and behaviors of managers in its national companies. Nationally influenced behavioral characteristics become an ingrained part of each company's "way of doing things" and shape its international organization structure and processes.

Competition in Business

Competition keeps markets efficient, prices low, and players lean but companies that don't innovate lose a critical source of future competitive advantage.

Foreign competition is growing. Technology is flattening. Be competitive and challenge foreign companies in global markets.

We must be competitive to survive. Competition is imposed on us by a world that has shrunk to a global market and we find ourselves trading in that market.

Changing world economies, changing prospects of access to world markets, new technologies and its changing implementation can affect the competitive edge.

There is a misunderstanding that companies working in emerging markets want tech that's a generation back. That is not true they want the most sophisticated technologies to have competitive advantage.

These are few concerns that are vocalized by the global players in businesses. Countries must equip themselves with the information, knowledge and the discipline necessary to develop their competitive edge to face the 21st Century. This has become imperative due to mega-trends emerging in the past decade: free trade in a global market; and rapid changes in technology and communications; and economic groupings such as the European Union.

Competitive Edge. The competitive edge in terms of sharpness, vigor of competition suggests action for growth, innovation and value creation. Companies, workgroups and individuals that master the competitive edge will build a more sustainable core. While our primary focus will be on business activity, our perspectives will also be relevant to leaders of other kinds of institutions as well — educational, governmental and social. This is giving rise to a new common sense model. We all perceive and act based on "common sense" assumptions about the world around us and the requirements to achieve our goals. Every major technology shift has produced a fundamentally new common sense model. Our goal is to understand and describe key elements of the new common sense model emerging from technology innovations — especially the invention of the microprocessor and PC, Internet and cellular technology, other biometric and ID technologies such as RFID, etc.

The competitive edge focuses on four different domains of human action — social, enterprise, market and learning. The social domain involves the complex relationships between how we define our individual identities and the forms of social participation that we pursue to shape these identities. The enterprise domain looks at how we organize to create economic value and how we define the boundaries of these economic entities. The market domain explores how we compete and collaborate on a global scale to create, deliver and capture economic value. The learning domain seeks to describe how we learn, with particular emphasis on the interaction between individual learning and group learning. The second and third are explicitly important to us for achieving competitive advantage in businesses; but we cannot undermine the importance of learning experiences and the social factor.

Complex dynamic loops shape the evolution of each domain and the interdependencies across domains. We believe that the biggest opportunities will arise where the competitive edges of these four domains interact and generate tensions that need to be resolved. Secondly, we need to understand how the four long-term global forces of public policy, technological innovations, demographic, and culture interact with the four above-mentioned domains:

- Public policy about economic and social policies for globalization, and policies about removing barriers to entry and competition in domestic and world markets.
- Technological innovations at three levels: a) the continuing improvement in price/performance in digital hardware building blocks and new techniques for designing, building and delivering software; b) the changing architectures for organizing these hardware and software building blocks; c) the movement into new arenas of these components and architectures (e.g., the mobile Internet, smart objects, bioinformatics and telematics).
- Demographic — the changing demographics around the globe is a powerful force to determine the type and

volume of consumerism and businesses. One size fit all approach is changing due to exposure to global products and services as well as different lifestyles. Now business practices are changing to address the needs of specific demographics which have huge segmented markets such as youth, the senior citizens, high-end consumers and low-end consumers. Since these segmented markets across the globe is one huge market in itself.

- Cultural force, i.e. the emergence of different global cultures such as youth cultures, consumerism, the growth of the new middle class, creative class, and the growing importance of religion in cultures around the world. These do impact the public policies for global enterprises and globalization whether it is bigger issues of oil embargo, food sanctions, or nuclear energy; or lesser issues of food fads, clothing fashions, cellular phone, and PCs.

Creating Value. Effective strategies will be needed to create value. These will bring together four management imperatives — Focus, Accelerate, Strengthen and Tie together (FAST strategies). Business enterprises will need to develop new approaches and tools to fit in the evolving global competitive environment, and to make progress in terms of creating value as the pace of change accelerates.

The conventional economic wisdom about what creates a competitive industry is natural resources, abundant labor pool, and favorable business environment. But it consistently ignores or underestimates the effects of local markets in fostering a global competitive advantage

Harvard business professor Porter's research (2005) has shown that factors such as the availability of natural resources and favorable labor costs decline in importance as value added activities increase. In a modern skill-based economy the single most important element that drives a competitive industry is the existence of a demanding domestic market. Local market challenges increase competitive pressure on companies in that market, which then puts those companies in a better position to compete globally. Additionally, the particular demands of the home market have a disproportionately large effect on how companies interpret customer requirements and develop strategy.

On the other hand, the global competitive edge can grow, when not only there is global demand but also two countries are in the race to win such as China and India competing in the global market for outsourcing and offshoring; though either of them can win depending on its strengths. But in the process, their weaknesses may get sharpened (improved upon) to compete further. China is educating more and more of its people in English speaking to compete for BPOs; developing software skills to compete with India, and making Chinese learn western management techniques to compete with the western business counterparts.

Jackson et al. (2004) argue that the old business process paradigms are no longer tenable. Continuous improvements and other "revolutionary" new models that have arisen to take their place over the past several decades have proven to be stopgap measures at best. Yet, one undeniable truth has emerged from all these is that to survive in today's global market-place, a company must perform like a world class competitor. Survival in the new world business order requires a clear understanding of changing customer needs coupled with the ability to translate those needs quickly and efficiently into products or services. Achieving the competitive edge helps them make world class performance a reality in their organizations.

There are concerns about the strategies for the corporate competitive advantage. How do corporations — old and new, large and small — stay competitive? Is innovation the key, or is it product quality, customer service, or institutional knowledge? Competition keeps markets efficient, prices low, and players learn but companies that don't innovate lose a critical source of future competitive advantage. Is innovation a function of research & development or are corporate culture and connectivity the key factors? Can the innovative spirit be acquired? What type of leadership fosters the creativity and risk-taking that allow established companies to continually reinvent them?

Entrepreneurship is vital to the global economy. So how do emerging entrepreneurs and established business families create and sustain their competitive edge? How should they adapt to today's rapidly globalizing world? The periodic emergence of business tycoons, who build new brands and business empires, changes the way we do business and understand the markets.

Strategic alliances of enterprises playing significant role in achieving competitive advantage has been emphasized by the researchers, and that alliances provide a platform for parent organizations to access other's resources and capabilities (Hamel, 1991; Grant,1996; Kogut, 1988; Anand & Khanna, (2000). Strategic alliances represent a type of inter-firm cooperative arrangements aimed at achieving the partners' strategic objectives (Das & Teng, 1998). *In fast-changing global markets, companies have become more interdependent and strategic partnerships have become essential to build and maintain competitive strength.* Organizations are motivated to form alliances for efficient development of firm's resources from a resource-based perspective. Companies may form alliances in which both partners have clear learning objectives to achieve long-term competitiveness.

Due to the increasing interdependence, companies have to develop the ability to build, maintain and manage their alliance relationships effectively. *Thus, cooperative strategies have become more common than competition to achieve competitive advantage.* In an era, where globalization drivers such as market, competition, government, and cost drivers (Yip, 1995; Ghauri, 1999) are forcing companies to search for external resources, a drastic change has occurred in the use of strategic alliances, and the number of alliances including joint ventures has increased manifold. Although the number is increasing, *the failure rate in coalition is high, as well. The reason is that coalition partners involved in relationship are facing difficulties in managing conflicts and adapting to environmental changes.*

The capabilities to manage strategic change are a crucial asset to competitive performance. An underlying premise is that effective inter-organizational alliances are associated with selection of appropriate partners who possess necessary resources (Sarkar et al., 2001) and learning to manage the alliance relationships to explore and exploit alliance resources. High interaction and communication between organizations increases information flow that increases the boundary permeability to the partners' resources. The differences in partner skills and knowledge provide the catalyst for learning. Hence, information flow offers an opportunity for organizational learning. Organizational learning has impact on company's performance.

Sustaining competitive edge is also important. US Government White paper on outsourcing and offshoring (May 11, 2004) presented by Senators is concerned about losing America's competitive edge in technology research and development through offshore and outsourcing. It further stated that,...... "the fact is, unknown to most workers, our economy and the global economy as a whole is undergoing fundamental structural changes. Most American companies engaged in offshoring think they are doing what they need to do to survive. While American companies may be improving their individual competitiveness in the short term, they may be collectively undermining America's and their own competitiveness for the long haul. Bit by bit, we're not just moving good jobs overseas, but we may be transporting big blocks of our innovation infrastructure, the talent and technology that fueled our record setting growth and prosperity in the 1990's".

"There has been little informed discussion of the fundamental long term challenge of offshoring high end engineering, research and development jobs. Nor have many acknowledged how our nation's irresponsible fiscal policy has undermined US competitiveness. The debate needs to focus on our own culpability and not simply decry other countries and their industries for rising to challenge us in the global economy. We cannot afford to idly stand by as we face the loss of parts of our innovation infrastructure — labor, capital, knowledge, technology, and plants – and with it the engine of job creation. Nor can we afford to build walls around our borders. *To save American jobs, we need to rise to the competition and grow through innovation.* There are no shortcuts, no silver bullets."

".....America is at its best when we are challenged. Over three hundred years we have assembled the most entrepreneurial and competitive workforce in the world. We are a confident and optimistic people. We love competition and rise to meet it. We are leaders and innovators. *We have established the basic rules of the game in which we are now* facing fierce competition — free enterprise, respect for the individual, and the rule of law.

That we now are facing fierce competitors is a sign that our values and policies have *succeeded.* We have fought for these values and they have now taken root throughout the world. Now we find that others can challenge us and occasionally even win. Our response to this must be what it has always been — to get to work, to be practical, to do what we have the power to do — to compete, and to continue to fight for the values and policies that have made this international competition possible".

It is argued by business professionals that organizations seek to achieve a sustained advantage in an increasingly competitive and geographically diverse market-place. Consequently, having a global orientation is no longer a luxury, but a necessity for economic survival in a large number of industries. *The primary motivations driving the globalization of the company are the comparative and competitive advantages that are gained by the integration of various value-added activities performed throughout the organization.*

They suggest that inherent organizational complexity necessitates the development of a new set of competencies that would engender a global market advantage. Presumably, this global market advantage would be associated with positive strategic and financial returns.

It is argued that market openness associated with globalization has increased the speed, frequency and magnitude of access to worldwide markets, including all tangible and intangible aspects of commerce, by a new and more diverse set of competitors. The motivations and drivers that engender fundamental changes in the industry structure include market factors, cost sensitivity, governmental influences, and competitive considerations. These factors have influenced the convergence of consumer expectations which, in turn, elicit responses to provide for these requirements.

The practice of getting competitive edge through partnership deals with the competitors is the new practice for business competition. Increasingly one finds that the *competition brings the best out of people and companies.* While some individuals stress themselves for higher productivity and results, others use creative methods to be productive. Information explosion means that your methods and techniques of competitive advantage would not remain inimitable for long. Hence, *companies need to be promoting continuous innovation in order to maintain sustained competitive advantage over the competition.*

Often best of the companies sometimes are found reacting to the competition. However, increased information means that these companies are able to react to competition at much faster rate decreasing the innovation edge to the innovator. Hence, the emphasis on continuous innovation by companies and promotion of sustained innovation culture in companies.

To take examples, Microsoft was found to be slow in reacting to Google's popular search engine and desktop search tools. However, once recognized as competitive threat, Microsoft was quick to react, launching its own similar tools. All this competition has led to development of Internet technologies with 'virtual office for users on net' and framework for Internet tools, ushering in a whole new paradigm of Internet usage and environments.

Similarly, on the hardware front, the passion for GHz and single-handed focus to pursue advanced semiconductor technologies led Intel to vigorously pursue the path, only to be hit by thermal limitations. This gave Advanced Micro Devices much needed leeway in promoting its own imitating processors in market with much success. The competition then led to both the companies competing hard with advanced 64 bit architecture technologies, dual core technology, the revolutionary virtualization technology and the next generation security technology and all this after increasing the performance of the processors to 3x in the time period.

Partnership deals with the competitors and the industry leader could also blunt the competitive edge of other competitors. Google and Dell partnership deal in May 2006 could blunt Microsoft's competitive edge.

Google and Dell partnership means millions of Dell computers will leave the factories with Google software already installed, an advantage that could widen the usage of the products and provide another boost to Google's already rapidly growing profits. So far it has to rely on users downloading its software from the Internet. Dell will install Google's desktop search software and its toolbar while preserving a space for the search engine in a side panel of Microsoft's Internet Explorer 6 browser. The home page on the browser will also be programmed to go to a Web page co-branded by Dell and Google, providing another springboard to feature advertising.

Second time in two weeks, Dell has aligned itself with a company that's posing a threat to an industry leader. Dell— the world's largest computer maker announced it would start using some processing chips made by Advanced Micro Devices Inc., which has been chipping away at the market share of Intel Corp.

We observe, the companies strive for, and gain global market competitive advantage through alliances of strategic partnerships, through business innovations in technology and management; and by creating values for their businesses. A top industry leader would combine all the three approaches. Take the example; the Steel business tycoon L.N. Mittal has achieved the top global leadership in Steel business in 2006 by combining the three approaches. More and more of the world's best companies rely on a common understanding of the companies' operations strategy throughout the organization. Building competitive advantage through operations, cuts through the rhetoric and provides practical tools and concepts for building sound operating strategies that work.

MNC in developed countries have some options to respond to competition from emerging multinationals. Emerging multinationals may have orthodox business models but they could be more innovative and effective. The MNC can analyze their advantages and anticipate how they (emerging) can transform their industry. Emerging multinationals are their challengers. MNC should boost their R&D and ally with the emerging rivals rather than let a future global rival build share, scale and handsome profits uncontested. Many MNC make better use of Chinese and Indian engineers, factories, and suppliers based in those countries. They thus neutralize an emerging challenger's low-cost advantage. Leading companies in developing countries can be great partners. They know the terrain and real market needs at home and in other key emerging growth markets. MNC can leverage their low cost resources by collaborating with them on product development. If an emerging rival has a clear advantage in a segment; it is time to exit, or form a joint venture and still make profit by selling expertise or services.

Business Innovations

Business is being re-invented in global context. Creativity and innovation are both defining how we compete and re-define who will own and control the greatest market opportunities in the world. This is true for both online and offline. Those *businesses that can re-invent themselves, change the rules of an industry by accepting change itself, define new markets; and offer entirely new ways of doing business will not only compete but break away from competition itself.* Those that can not change practices will be left behind far more quickly. Businesses are getting continually redefined, and reinventing new ways of doing business in the global market place is no longer an option—it is utter necessity.

Of course, triumph today doesn't guarantee success tomorrow. In this new world, CEOs must now force their organizations to stretch, think and take risks. They must cut deals that take them beyond the traditional rules of competition, attracting and hiring creative strategic thinkers who can re-invent the rules of their industries—in real time, or watch as their businesses become re-invented around them. *The external growth through partnerships, through M&A, strategic alliances, and creative deal-making is now an essential ingredient for continuously reinventing any business.* As Garnick (2006) pointed, if you are reinventing through acquisition, you cannot change a little at a time, you have to change the entire DNA of the company. Such wholesale change can accelerate through strong acquisition strategy.

Henig Peter (2006) points that by reinventing products, divisions, and major technology shifts in an enterprise, you can change the business practices. Traditionally, the reinvention would have occurred due to changing market conditions or market competition. But since a decade back, the change is accelerated due to globalization and with that reinvention is accelerated also.

Reinvention is focusing on best business practices to retrain workforce to remain competitive, re-invent the talent with new skills, re-tooling Board of Directors to meet new business and governance challenges, and the use of mergers and acquisitions to re-engineer business product lines and re-invent management teams in the process. To transform a company, it is necessary to reinvent the top leadership talent; continually developing leadership throughout the company and even bringing management from the outside to ensure right leadership and new perspective for the company's culture. *The corporate structure, board structure, accounting methods, reporting processes are all getting re-invented to fit in the global practices of standardizing. The essence of re-invention is innovation, invention and risk-taking in order to take the businesses to the next level of success.*

Reinvention of businesses at home will have the impact across global businesses. The willingness of corporate culture to accept change with honesty and rigor will determine the success or failure of reinvention. *We need to rebuild a business culture with new global point of views.*

Lowe Ken (2006) advocates that business managers have to change their views of the future business practices and let go how things were done in the past. We have to reinvent and reinvest in our organizations that never stop evolving in the global contexts. It is the sense of possibilities and diversifications in businesses; and businesses setting higher bars within an organization will be significant for consistent and sustainable re-invention. The organizations must set the bars high and understand what key measures of success exist to help define companies' re-invention and future opportunities for growth.

The pressure to change has become more significant, whether because new business models are coming up, new products are disrupting or business intermediaries are getting less important. "*We have to engage in restless self-renewal because the sands of time are always shifting. Self-renewal is one of the defining elements of building and rebuilding any competitive global business into the 21st century and beyond.*" (Lowe Ken 2006).

The globalization of businesses, of workplace, and how businesses in the future will be re-built and re-invented on global scale are top concerns of enterprises these days. Business strategies have to be invented and re-invented fast to serve the needs of the global customer base, manufacturing products from facilities across the globe by operations and research.

What is significant is *how these business practices are communicated to consumers and businesses worldwide due to changing modes of communication and also due to impact of practices changing in other domains. The significance lies in thinking globally and coping with global trends by capacity building and improved management techniques and facing challenges of changing business practices and redefining and re-inventing businesses.*

We suggest a few pointers, a few supporting stories and news in the media to highlight both the trends and its learning process.

Let us take the topic to integration and collaboration. Innovation is not about services and products, it is about business models. Products and services can be copied, so what's going to be different is the differentiated business model. By collaborating, you can learn quicker and do things faster. It's a way to accelerate the speed. The faster you can innovate, the longer you will be able to sustain operating margins over a period of time. In the past products were important, now innovation is becoming important.

Companies do not have enough scale to do everything on their own. There is tremendous pressure on companies to innovate; otherwise they will miss the opportunity. It was best for IBM to partner with Lenovo; when they saw the PC industry move to consumers. IBM wanted to get into PC components. They created a collaborative model, so in spite of getting higher bids from financial players, they partnered with Lenovo to participate in the China market. If you are not innovating, you are getting into what an author has described as 'commodity hell'.

When IBM had a PC business, it was not very easy for them to enter the consumer business. They were no doubt very good in the enterprise business. But PC is a volume business, so you have to enter the consumer sector to survive. After the acquisition, they have brought in competitiveness in the industry. Now IBM and Lenovo have a win-win situation, they have common competition, and they have complementary businesses. Their teams work together in China.

There is demand for hardware and software, and as they advance, there is much more emphasis on services. As economies evolve, consumers spend more, so consumer credit demand increases and that creates more demand for crunching consumer data; and more systems need to be created to support these activities. As companies get sophisticated, they demand more sophisticated systems. It's a big opportunity, and IBM wants to make sure that the entire set of solutions to companies are provided, right from PC based support to back end. For example, the Chinese banks are demanding extremely sophisticated stuff, so IBM has to take Chinese people to US and train them in US banks, so that they could see and learn the very best.

Innovation has changed, in 90s it involved dealing with vast technological shifts that disrupted and threatened companies. Today, it means building the process that promotes an idea generating culture. By understanding how social, commercial, and physical networks behave, innovators can develop new tactics. Innovation sprouts from the fertile ground of inquiry.

Most people view innovation predominantly as a creative exercise. What do today's innovation practitioners think it makes enterprises to be innovative? More than creativity, what makes a company innovative is a climate that continuously fosters innovation. This is a shift in thinking from popular belief.

The new communication practice for creativity and encouraging innovations in business organizations is 'Building Innovation Labs' which is important. It is a space, away from the work area and exclusively provided by the organizations to let people focus on new projects, and to encourage creativity and new design strategies throughout the organizations. People go there to meet people and converse about their own ideas and others' ideas and interaction generate new ideas. Procter & Gamble calls it Gym, Eastman Kodak – Steelcase, Samsung and IBM have innovation labs. Samsung's innovative spirit is driven by 17 R&D centers and 6 design centers worldwide. IBM research foundation is in wide array of scientific disciplines, award-winning researchers and global labs. Over the years, they have expanded to include challenging ideas from their colleagues in academic, industry and government research centers as well as from their clients. Intel has innovation labs in China and India. Motorola, HP and many other are companies are following this practice of setting up innovation labs.

Having a particular innovation to work on, an inter-disciplinary research team is set up. They brainstorm, they generate, work on new ideas exclusively in the innovation labs away from the mainstream business; till an innovation seems on sight to be further developed. This is an interdisciplinary approach to innovation and to the task of improving the ability of small and medium-sized companies to exploit new technologies and management tools. Brainstorming and countering negativity is important for business innovations

Operating globally involves more than reaching out to far-flung locales for needy customers, low-cost labor, and ready capital. *Increasingly, large companies are also globalizing innovation as well.* A few examples: Jeff Immelt from GE is reaching out to try multiple ideas. It first built an international team of researchers in Germany, China, India and the USA to build a better wind turbine. A.G. Lafley from Procter and Gamble has improved R&D productivity by co-developing brands with other companies from around the globe. Chinese engineers in the Beijing lab from Motorola conceived a Linux-based mobile phone, now a crucial part of its software strategy. The revolutionary (non-processor frequency based) technology behind Intel's Centrino wireless technology was developed in Haifa, Israel where challenging orthodox idea is rooted in the culture.

Swiss-based Novartis is developing new medicines in a Shanghai laboratory, specializing in ancient remedies. Dutch electronics giant Philips got the idea for a core product, their new home heart defibrillator "HeartStart", via a US-based research lab. *Accessing the brains everywhere in the world is paying of for these companies apparently.*

Acquisitions and mergers is emerging as new strategy and practice for worldwide growth. The external growth through partnerships, through M&A, strategic alliances, and creative deal-making is now an essential ingredient for continuously reinventing any business. M&A also creates diversifications in businesses both globally and at home and that widens the scope of the businesses.

Indian companies also see Acquisitions and Mergers as new strategy and practice. For decades, the corporate India has been sticking close to home and protecting its markets from foreign incursions. Now, Indian companies are scouting for international acquisitions and mergers for wider growth. The trend is changed by economic liberalization policies, cheaper capital, low Indian interest rates and low (though it is changing with changed economic scenarios) global interest rates. At the same time Indian Government has liberalized restrictions in tapping international debt markets and the boom in Indian stock market is also providing an easy source of funds. Over and above, the new breed of Indian executive is leading this practice. They are educated at western management schools, trained in multinationals and global in outlook. Their approach marks a radical departure from conventional approach to oppose any market opening moves and market economy. Now some of the same companies with younger generations with global outlook at the helm, support proposals that would open Indian economy wider and wider.

Indian companies are getting strong, cost-efficient and with larger opportunities are acquiring companies to build their own competence and scalability. Most of the acquisitions have been so far for small companies. But as Indian companies achieve global scale; their acquisition sizes will also grow. Indian companies are getting confident of their ability to manage global enterprises. By pushing overseas, many Indian companies hope to gain expertise, build brands, and add scale to set themselves up in business abroad and competition at home.

In India, the recent changing business practices by enterprises are widening the scope of their businesses by diversifications. In 2006, the big business houses like Reliance Industries have announced their diversification in retail, agriculture—agro-processing, and petroleum and refineries. Reliance capital is foraying into energy and power, entertainment, communications, telecom and Real estate. Bharti is into telecom mainly but diversifying in Real estate. Zee tele is foraying into entertainment and Real estate. The United Breweries is getting into Airlines beside spirit business. Many other companies are diversifying and thus expanding with domestic or global partners and also finding business scope in other countries. Such as in 2006, the foreign investment is opened in retail and Real estate, in 2004-5 foreign funding and equity for airlines was opened.

This has been possible because of changed practices about economic reforms, liberalization and opening of certain areas for foreign funding and equity as communicated by government policies and the businesses accepting the globalization challenges.

Enterprise Architecture (EA): The concept of enterprise architecture (EA) is old, the position of enterprise architect is new, and has become relevant recently with the emergence of Web services and the move towards service-oriented architectures that enable IT components to be used in multiple applications. Demand for EA and system development is rising in cost effective markets. EA is a comprehensive framework used to manage and align an organization's business processes, Information Technology (IT) software and hardware, people, operations and projects with the organization's overall strategy. This certainly leads to streamlining and optimum utilization of resources.

Prof. Christensen (2006) said, "Money is made by corporations that control the architecture of the system. GM made money through the artistry and expertise of the world's best designers. When a company does that, it outsources to its several vendors and suppliers to deliver better components through disintegrated architecture. In the process, vendors commoditize the product, while the corporations commoditize its customers. To make a 'foolproof and idiot simple product', corporations need to commoditize expertise instead of replicating expertise elsewhere. Corporations seeking to figure out their capabilities and inadequacies in accomplishing success need to focus on resources, processes and profit models. To do this, the top management needs to clearly articulate its priorities, he pointed out."

Restructuring corporate. The practices in restructuring plans of corporate are changing in context of changing technologies, globalization contexts and global businesses and diversification of businesses. Inefficient and expensive structure slows down decision-making and does not work in the digital age when products are being networked together is undergoing change. Communications has become more imperative among management, division heads, and other levels of senior and junior positions because of communication technologies facilitating interactions and also because of impact of changing communicatior and business practices worldwide. The interactions may be through formal and informal meetings. *The exchange of best practices and ideas must be shared which did not happen before.*

More crucial is when the restructuring plans are to be carried in global businesses in foreign countries. The role of foreign CEO is significant. Rather than isolating himself in the isolated suites, the practice is changing, he/she must mingle with the managers who are closer to the indigenous personnel who have more and close local insights about the business culture of their own company as well of other businesses in general. Foreign CEO has to be sensitive to the cultural divide and must respect the cultural differences, not necessarily to speak the language since he may not be adept in the nuances of the native language. So, he/she may concentrate more on the business than on language. If he has to restructure the plans, he must describe his strategy first to invite comments and suggestions, and once finalized; he has to be decisive to implement it. He must seek cooperation from management and staff to implement. *The emerging practice is to seek involvement and cooperation of office personnel.*

The companies doing global businesses must be staffed by international workforce. Any global model needs to be fueled by outstanding local insights. They know the consumers better than head quarters.

Indian companies are hiring specialists and local anchors in each country to help reconcile differences and conflicts since they find themselves ill-equipped to tackle diverse consumer and employee cultures in alien markets after the recent spate of mergers and acquisitions. Indian multinationals are now recruiting more locals at the front-end of the business in new global markets. "We are hiring talent from international business schools and training our employees to acquire a global mind-set. Indian business schools have not really paid much importance to exposing students to the elements of international businesses".

"There is a complete re-orientation happening within our company after becoming a global player," said Adi Godrej, promoter & chairman of Godrej Consumer. Financial sense is not enough to make a success of global mergers and acquisitions. Several M&As fail when diverse cultures fail to integrate, a KPMG study indicates.

Marico, in fact, held a global meet recently (2006) to discuss the relevance of the company values in a global market and expose people to diverse cultures. The integration of international managers plays a big factor in developing global expertise. Understanding how people think, work, eat, and interact in a foreign workplace is crucial to building a successful operation. There are positive aspects also. Cultural diversity has tremendous potential for innovation, arising from the presence of multiple perspectives.

"We were initially uncomfortable with the process-oriented systems and a lot of time and planning that people in organizations abroad did before taking on a new project. As Indian businesses, we have the practice of plunging into project head-on and taking decisions along the way."

MNC players are increasingly going for managers with a global mind-set, and recruiting local professionals to tide over cultural differences in various markets. Tata Motors, which took over Daewoo's commercial vehicle division, continues to let Korean managers run the place. "We decided against placing too many Indian managers at the place so as to let them integrate faster into the system and also draw from each other's strengths. We thought it better to let the company function as a part of the local economy," said a top company official.

People from different cultures tend to misunderstand each other's behaviors or stereotype people from other countries. It is essential to recognize the discrepancies between cultures in order to work together effectively.

Changing practices for risk management of devastation, disaster Management: We need to develop sustainable strategies to cope with them. "We cannot stop natural calamities, but we can and must better equip individuals and communities to withstand them. Those most vulnerable to nature's wrath are usually the poorest, which means that when we reduce poverty, we also reduce vulnerability."— UN Secretary General Kofi Annan, in a message to mark the International Day for Disaster Reduction, and on the heels of a devastating earthquake in Pakistan that left tens of thousands dead. The quake, which Pakistani President Pervez Musharraf's spokesman called the worst devastation in Pakistan's history, also killed many hundreds more in India. Mr. Annan noted the year's range of disasters from the massive Indian Ocean earthquake and tsunami, to the ravages of drought .and locusts in Africa, from the devastation caused by hurricanes and cyclones in the United States, the Caribbean and the Pacific to the heavy flooding across Europe and Asia. *Even microfinance can help empower those with little or no access to traditional financial institutions, thereby reducing disaster risk and improving disaster management.*

Beyond their obvious and painful effects on communities and families, such events can have devastating consequences for businesses. Many of them may not have any recovery plan and may not open again. In addition to natural disasters, businesses face panoply of growing operational risks in every day-to-day operations. The accounting scandals that destroy Enron, and WorldCom, the Internet interruptions lost business transactions and the computer viruses cause loss more than $13 billions a year. These risks multiply as companies move overseas. Insolvencies, protracted defaults, other creditors problems get difficult to handle in timely fashion across borders. Companies operations, payment problems with a single large foreign creditor can be potentially devastating in international trade without credit insurance.

Today, climate change is a fact and change presents us with both risk and opportunities. There is potential risk of climate change on the financial services and businesses. We need to identify environmental risks and help develop sustainable strategies to cope with them.

This exponential increase in the consequences of risk requires that corporations begin thinking of risk management in new ways. Corporate risks that have very high expected costs such as natural calamities but not likely to occur within any given time period needs more careful balancing of costs and benefits.

Earlier the cost of defective product may have been replacement of product, now it may mean costly multi-billion dollar class-action suit (such as for Viox medicine) and scathing media coverage which may imperil its whole business.

Therefore, the new strategy of risk assessment and management is important for businesses. *They adopt a strategy called 'enterprise risk management' (ERM) to improve their risk management capabilities*. ERM is method of assessing, preparing for, and responding to risk. It is a new way of thinking about risk and its challenges.

The risk managers need baseline facts to improve their risk calculations through data bases. They need to translate these vast arrays of information into actionable intelligence. They need adequate risk modeling tools. Newer causally based models offer substantial improvements over earlier statistically based models. Once knowledge and tools have been developed, there should be commitment.

Developing an effective ERM program is necessary though challenging in the new risk environments. First step is to define objectives that organizations can continue to fill both during and after a crisis. Second, demonstrate value, the cost of the program and its benefits for a range of potential risk scenarios. Third, focus the program on a few well defined goals. Even the most effective ERM program cannot achieve everything during the crisis period when many communication channels are impaired.

Your program should cover all aspects of strategic planning that are vital to the program's success such as clear assessment of the company's current risk management efforts, potential risks and associated costs company is likely to incur during crisis, the roadmap for implementing the ERM program. The specific resources required, the performance measurement mechanisms to be used; and the benefits that will accrue to the company and its stakeholders.

In May 2006, Mexico's $160 million bonds issue, to insure against earthquakes. This is the first attempt by a developing country to tap the world's capital markets in the event of natural disaster. México's has issued $ 160 Million catastrophe bonds to cover against the risk of earthquakes. These have been sold to institutional investors in USA and Europe. This will act like an insurance policy for the Mexican government. The investors are paying $160 million into a fund created by Swiss Re AG for the Mexican government. If an earthquake of a certain force hits in the designated areas of the country within the next three years then the Mexican government will get all the money. If it does not then the money is returned to the investors.

The Mexican bond is significant because it is the first time that a sovereign country has issued such catastrophe bonds or cat-bonds. It is also important because it is the first cat-bond to provide exposure to natural risks outside the developed world. The cat-bond market has developed slowly but steadily since 90s as insurers have used the capital-market instruments as an alternative to use their own balance sheets to covert the potentially huge cost of natural disaster like hurricane or earthquake, which could provoke massive insurance claims in the area.

This bond could be a harbinger of other issues by developing countries because it has the merit of unlocking funds immediately after a disaster for rebuilding.

The Commonwealth Telecommunication Organization (CTO) and the International Telecommunication Union (ITU) have organized the Using ICT for Effective Disaster Management Caribbean Forum 2006. The event took place between 26th & 28th September 2006 in Jamaica. The objective of this 'call for action' event was to provide the organizers with an opportunity to work with countries in the region to put in place the necessary platform for disaster prevention, preparedness and relief. This event will go beyond the abstract and look at practical ways through which disasters can be mitigated by using Information and Communication Technologies (ICT).

The event participants would discuss the role of ICTs and role of government, regulatory authorities, humanitarian organizations and telecommunication providers is disaster risk reduction.

This will build on the goals set by the World Conference for Disaster Reduction in Kobe, Japan in 2005, the conclusions of the World Summit on the Information Society, and the resolutions and programs adopted by ITU's World Telecommunication Development Conference that was held in Doha in March 2006. Refer Appendix 1 for CTO and ITU role.

Technology context is the most significant in business innovations. As we have observed through our detailed discussions about technology in Chapter 3; technology gave promise for the effective progress of businesses. Over the years Technology became complex. It was necessary to overcome the complexity. Technological processes were innovated to overcome the complexity.

All this has benefited consumers with new products and services, lower costs, higher performance and advanced features. Technology shifts are one of the factors to give competitive advantage to domestic market and facilitate globalization speedily and giving competitive advantage in the global markets also.

Education context. Globalization boost competition for workforce; therefore the education and skills to equip this workforce must improve upon and change with the demands of globalization whether it is IT, engineering, business education, entrepreneurship or even the languages to fit in with the changing roles. Teaching practices in business schools world around are changing. The focus is to make studies more on learning about global economy, learning entrepreneurship in globalization, technology and capital investment contexts and environments.

Learning entrepreneurship by imitation is another technique for business school students to learn entrepreneurship. It is hard to get students to learn what is involved in creating a company. 'Why not bring students to serial entrepreneurs'. The students are placed in growing companies and alongside high energy entrepreneurs who agree to work closely with the protégés.

Two top business schools, Insead of France and IESE of Spain are experimenting with 'European Entrepreneurship Accelerator program' created by Peter Zaboji, Julia Prats, and Heinrich Von Liechtenstein faculty from these two schools. They developed a 'demanding criteria' to select companies for the Accelerator Program – growth of at least 100 per cent a year, a strong business model and aspirations to grow into a strong pan-European or global company.

The executives at the company are vital for this program, particularly their willingness to work with the students and not just share with them entrepreneurial enthusiasm but company details also (Julia Prat).

The program calls for the students to take a few trips to the companies for personal meetings, but the companies and students communicate mostly via Internet and videoconferencing. Entrepreneurship Accelerator program takes the MBA education a step further than networking and business plan competitions. Small businesses and entrepreneurship are critical to economic growth. The program has started from Jan 06. The students in the program say, "It was valuable since you experience the high and lows of small-business reality under the mentorship of serial entrepreneur". "This is far cry from actually planning strategy and executing your recommendation with the CEO and staff."

MARKET SEGMENTS

Low-end Markets

Business practices are changing in the developing countries to focus on low-end market of poor in the urban and rural areas and the rural market itself. These practices have to focus on: a) market capacity, b) different type of consumers, c) different type of products and services fitting to rural tastes and needs, d) products and services of urban consumers but fitted into affordable price band of ruralites, and e) a huge segment of market.

Consumers in these markets have different characteristics, needs for different products and services, and in different price band which is affordable. The quality cannot be compromised, price must be affordable. These market demands can be met cost effectively by changing business practices. Secondly, creating awareness through cost-effective modes of advertising and marketing; through cost-effective channels of distribution and retail sale; and delivery of products and services in cost effective packaging can be done. Thirdly, the focus is on microfinance to let them buy these goods and services.

Special Segment Consumer Markets

Business Model for Rural markets. In developing countries, 70-80% of their population lives in rural areas. They have low connectivity with inadequate physical infrastructures such as roads, public transport, etc. They have low density of telephones and only some of them are exposed to electricity and TV, etc. It is only recently that businesses understand the importance of rural markets; these have been ignored so far. Now Rural Business models are being developed.

This model focuses on seven characteristics of rural markets and consumers: i) purchasing capability, ii) durable and non-durable consumer needs according to rural life styles. For example, they would need a different kind of food, different kind of soaps and detergents. Quite likely, there may not be any market for toilet tissue and paper napkins, iii) sachet economy will be the priority for durable consumer goods, iv) businesses need to tap the market for farm implements, accessories and farm goods and provide doorstep delivery system, v) delivery system is the most crucial part of the marketing strategies since villagers have low mobility, less knowledge and familiarity with the urban markets for purchasing and price negotiations. In the second phase of their marketing strategies the focus should be to, vi) enhance their purchasing power by providing micro-credit, vii) through micro-credit, businesses also capture some share of market for regular products and services in course of time and thus increasing their total market share.

Another peculiarity of the rural market will be the fast changing consumer scenarios due to their exposure to media channels of TV where they are exposed to lifestyles of various Indian regions and additionally to the global lifestyles and consumer goods. Therefore, the businesses need to consider this factor also. Business teams need to live with them for a while for having firsthand knowledge to understand the consumer dynamics for (their) consumer products and services.

Co-Creation Business Model is doing business with poor consumers with low purchasing capabilities. How to create markets for the poor who are at the bottom-of-the-Pyramid and who may be earning even less than few rupees/ a few cents a day? *We need different business model—the Co-Creation Business Model.*

They are the masses but they do need the basics and necessities of life and can buy according to, 'as and when and as much' they can spend for their needs. It is a mass market. As such the poor consumers' major demand is 'sachet economy'. The main strategies of this business model are: tap this mass market, and do marketing of products according to their lifestyles without encouraging materialistic consumerism, produce according to their low purchasing power, mobility and accessibility. Thus there are three essential dimensions of Co-Creation Business Model: i) produce products and services for the poor, low income masses matching their purchasing power and capabilities, ii) enhance their purchasing power by providing micro-credit, iii) through micro-credit, businesses also capture some share of market for regular products and services in course of time and thus increasing their total market share.

Prahalad (2004d) talks about the 'Invisible Market'. We need a new world economic order in which there is an invisible market constituency of these 5 billion poor people. In developing countries like India, China, Brazil, Mexico, Indonesia, Turkey, Russia, South Africa — they represent 70-75 per cent of the world population of poor.

If the poor, due to its limited purchasing power can buy small sachet of shampoo or small packets of food for a couple of servings such as quarter size or half-size bread loaves – then businesses should produce them, market them to this mass market. The demand is there and it will continue in the same proportion but in different time-scale since the poor can spend limited amount on a specific consumer product at a point of time. If a business can sell cheaper the same product without packaging frills, then produce and market the same to this segment of market. In short, this segment of market has demand for the product but it has to be marketed differently. The poor want value for their money; and businesses can deliver that by marketing differently and in turn they have the business of the 70-80 per cent consumers segments to make profits.

Invisible market of rural and poor consumers. Prahlad (2004c) talks about the invisible market of consumers (both rural and poor) and how to connect with it. As a practice in recent years, Hindustan Lever in India has made it compulsory for a person who joins the company in regular job to live in villages for three months at a stretch before starting work in the company. It does not matter who you are and at what level you join. You have to develop a project in that village, so that you are working closely with the local people. Why? The company wants you to understand your consumers and be in close interaction with the villagers to assess their needs, tastes, preferences, and affordability. So that it can co-create product accordingly for this segment, which is a huge market. Further, to connect with the poor consumers, every year for one day, everyone from chairman to down, have to get out of the office and visit a poor-family consumer. Then, after the visit, when they come back, they write a report about what they have learned and how it will impact upon management and product development practices.

Generally, top management and employees are disconnected with the poor and rural consumers. And there is a huge disconnect with all managers and not just senior managers, in multinational companies and five billion potential consumers in low income and poor. Because we do not interact with poor, we do not know how they live. Other big companies are also following the example. Most of them are even encouraging their senior managers to visit their targeted villages to have face-to-face and hand-on experience of the feasibility and marketability of their products. They work on the presumptions that sitting in air-conditioned offices in the cities far from the villages cannot give them reality check on the rural markets and low-end markets.

ITC company's e-Choupal program in India has contributed to overall programs of development. e-Choupal has helped increase the incomes and productivity of millions of farmers by giving them more direct access to markets, as well as pricing and product information, via village-based Internet kiosks. e-Choupal is now expanding its service to include education. It has opened 100 e-Choupals in Andhra Pradesh in 2006.

There are other examples from India such as affordable small car Maruti, and with bank loans, the middle class could afford it. Maruti Udyog Ltd. of India tapped the huge middle class market and boosted its sales. Another in the pipeline and planned to be cheaper than this is Tata's starter family car likely to hit the market in 2008. This is aimed at the huge lower middle class market. The person from lower middle class needs to buy two-wheeler scooter for his work commute. May be he can afford to buy it through easy loan from the bank. He wants to take his family for drive and leisure activities. He takes his wife and two children on the scooter – all four on the pinion. Rattan Tata is concerned about seeing the family safely in a small car rather all four on the pinion of the two-wheeler scooter! We have to have a starter car competing with the scooter prices but certainly with more safety. These two kinds of markets, middle-class and lower-middle-class consumers have huge potential market for these two different categories of cars — when they are available at affordable prices and when the purchasing capacity of the consumers is augmented.

If the poor are poorly served and there are ways to serve them better, that's going to create benefits to the poor. This new market requires partnerships not only with other companies but also with local communities, non-profit organizations. Corporations have to deal with them to create a much more inclusive and interesting business model.

How do we sell to the poor? Create capacity to buy through easy loan and hire- purchase system. Earlier, the poor could take loans from the moneylenders but in the process, they suffered the exploitation from the moneylenders paying exorbitant rates of 500 per cent interest. But now the banks can give them micro-loans at 10 per cent and develop their capacity to buying, saving and consuming simultaneously. The corporate can let them buy their products on hire-purchase system. They are paying in easy installments and consuming simultaneously.

Co-Creation theory advocates that consumer is supreme and pivotal for product demands and the market is co-created through consumer demands and expectations whether consumer is elite or down the pyramid. There are elite and informed consumers, and then there are poor and not so informed consumers who are at the bottom-of-the-pyramid. There are urban (both elite and poor) consumers, and consumers in rural areas. All these four categories have different levels of exposure to information channels. All are important for the business to develop product and market segments for the same.

London Ted (2005) points that when MNCs go overseas; they typically look for customers that are the most familiar. As a result, in the developing world, they tend to target the wealthy. But now there has been increasing interest in reaching into the second tier of the pyramid that you could call the emerging middle class, maybe 1.5 billion people. These are people that are beginning to get some wealth but are still in the middle class in these developing countries.

What they have not targeted is the 4 billion plus people in the base of the socio-economic pyramid. The focus is on what it takes for an organization to profitably, or in a self-sustaining way serve this market in a manner that is environmentally sensitive and culturally appropriate. This latter component is crucial, as we really believe the models that are going to work in BOP (bottom-of-pyramid) markets need to be economically viable but also need to address for social and environmental performance. They tend to pay a premium for services that are offered to people in the same general geographic location who are wealthier.

The changing practices in businesses are that a Big Corporation Think Small. The marketing products to rural markets and poor who are bigger consumer markets are the changing trends by bigger companies through sachet economy. Newer business practices are being explored to fit in this market and get the best consumer response and profits. Prof. Christensen (2006) commenting on this trend said, " There were three ways of doing this: One, by making a complicated product affordable; two, by creating low-end disruption through low-cost products; and three, by executing new disruption by penetrating frontier markets where no corporation had ventured before." Elaborating this he said, "Intel had developed the Celeron chip to storm the low-end market with a complicated yet affordable product. In doing this, it had addressed over-served customers with a lower-cost business model instead of bringing a better product in an established market. Likewise, Canon unleashed low-end disruption through low-cost products by introducing small, smart copiers with better scanning."

He further commented that companies could also grow big by penetrating unexplored frontier markets as had been done by a Chinese manufacturer of microwave ovens at a low-price point of $39, in the process, bringing in 160 million new customers. It is not low-cost labor, but non-consumption that creates a market for big volumes and success. Corporations seeking to figure out their capabilities and inadequacies in accomplishing success need to focus on resources, processes and profit models. To do this, the top management needs to clearly articulate its priorities.

The retail market strategies are changing; they are focusing on rural markets and low-end income groups in urban areas. Since in developing countries, majority of population live in rural areas and a bigger segment in urban is low end.

There's also a question of population shifts and tough competition from local brands in the rural market, which baffles the urban-based marketing people. Rural consumers are far less homogeneous than their urban counterparts and differ from region to region. The Indian rural market of India consists of about 70-80 per cent of the population of the country but it does differ in its various regions.

Apparently in terms of the number of people, the Indian rural market is almost twice as large as the entire US market or Russia. This market is large, but scattered and diverse. It exhibits linguistic, regional and cultural diversities and economic disparities, and hence, it can easily be considered as being more complex than the market of a continent as a whole.

The prices of rural marketing pose many problems due to the vastness of the country and a high potential for providing an effective marketing system. Another myth is that their purchasing power is low. Christensen remarked that at 15.6 million 'middle class' households, the rural areas compared well with 16.4 million urban households.

For the same income level, disposable surplus in villages is much higher than in urban India, he said. Companies have begun offering urban-like shopping experience at venues where rural business transactions are undertaken. But rural consumers are more value-conscious than the urban consumer and market watchers are wondering whether marketers can retain the interest once the novelty runs out. As a long-term measure, these initiatives will bear fruit, but experts say there's no concerted effort by other companies to make in-roads.

Companies need to step up investments in wider distribution systems. "The question is what attempts are being made to localize marketing strategies and offer products fine-tuned to meet their tastes. The rural markets will be more complicated than the urban markets. But the number of people who will go to the malls to buy big-ticket items, where deliberation is usually done will be fewer in volume terms."

But the problems are larger that stem from the under-developed markets. The awareness of rural consumers about products is obviously lesser than the urban markets and therefore, more purchasing power is not enough. Also, urban and semi-urban-based salesmen are not able to tap the full potential in the villages. We have strongly suggested that marketers select and employ educated unemployed from villages and venture into wider areas.

Another changing practice in India for rural markets: "With the high-level involvement of CII (Confederation of Indian Industries) and different wings of governments and panchayats, we may be able to transform the image of rural India. The government has identified 846 products for which the business community could have a partnership with panchayats for establishing rural business hubs based on Chinese model. The rural business hubs scheme, launched in 2004, to be set up in partnership with CII would upgrade and upvalue the skills and the products made by the villagers. This is a new experiment based on P4 model (public-private-panchayat-partnership) and so far 72 companies have shown interest in setting up such business hubs.

A total of 31 MOU have been signed towards the rural business hubs (RBH) project involving Reliance, Tatas, Coco-Cola, ITC, Mahindra and Mahindra and Microsoft among others. RBH is a P4 model initiative wherein the industry will be involved with rural resources and skills to develop products of internationally accepted quality. "Ministry is ensuring the convergence of the Central Government and the State Government scheme relevant to various RBHs and there will be 55 of them very soon" (News item 2006).

Rural Markets and Rural Consumption in India: Emerging Practices

Many Indian businesses are going rural. In a bid to expand their market base, companies are now exploring the rural hinterland. Hindustan Lever (HLL) for one has been continuously strengthening its marketing network in the villages and is producing goods to suit the needs and budgets of rural consumers. Along with soaps, detergents and toothpaste, ITC's — Sagar sells almost everything — TVs, DVD players, pressure cookers, room heaters, watches, sewing machines and grinders. Farmers can also buy motorbikes, or even tractors. ITC has launched its own rural range of clothing and shoes too —tailored for the village folk. ITC officials claim that the mall is doing brisk business. Others are Pepsi Foods, Tata Kisan Sansar, EID Parry

— the list is expanding everyday. They are all taking the rural route to expand their market base, as well as to procure raw materials for their agro ventures. Many companies are setting up contract farming in the villages. This business plan benefits the company as well as the farmers. One, farmers learn new and improved ways of growing food. Secondly, sale of their produce is assured.

A larger number of Indians live in villages but what is significant is that villages have undergone drastic changes in the post-reform era. While the trickling-down effect of higher GDP growth and a low inflation rate have improved the economic conditions of the villagers, the exposure to new products through media especially broadcasting channels has changed their consumption patterns also. The delivery of those goods through the efforts of the businesses in various areas, and in different ways further facilitates those consumption patterns.

Indian villages have become more health conscious and are now spending more on medicines — share of medical expenses in monthly consumption expenditure has increased from 5.7 per cent in 1997 to 6.8 per cent in 2002. Despite the fact, government highly subsidizes or provides free delivery of health and medicines to the rural consumers. They are spending higher amount on clothing also. Their conventional food consumption patterns have also changed from home-made lassi to Pepsi and other soft drinks. Higher expenditure on healthcare will keep them fit, but Indian households are no longer prepared to ignore the worldly comforts either. The most dramatic change has been witnessed in the non-durable consumer goods sector. They would like to buy TV, VCR, DVD, washing machines and refrigerators for personal comforts. They would be equally interested to buy tractors and other agriculture machinery to enhance their agriculture productivity.

It may be the demonstration effect caused by the opening up of the economy to the global market. But the fact remains that their expenditure on consumer goods, services and consumer durables and non-durables has increased sharply during the period. The business model of co-creation and marketing strategies targeted to this segment vide the above mentioned three-tier efforts would increase markets for the businesses.

Businesses are built on developing the capacity of the poor. There are 300 million cellphones in China or 40 million cellphones in India and they are adding 1.5 million subscribers per month. They are not all in the hands of the rich. In fact, in developing countries, the poor skilled or unskilled in business of plumber, electrician, carpenter or vegetable vendor are utilizing it for connectivity for their business. Diffusion of cellphones is creating business connectivity beside social change. The cellphone businesses are (being) built around the consumer demand and experience of the poor people. In these countries they have the growth opportunity (Narula 2005).

Microfinance practices are changing

As we discussed above, the awareness of poor, low-income and rural people for a comfortable lifestyle, and use of technology for agri-production and other small-scale industries, and entertainment is sufficiently aroused by media and interpersonal advertisements and campaigns. The awareness thus created demands the products and services. Businesses must make efforts to increase markets among this segment of consumers by sachet techniques and other appropriate emerging business models. The significant point in this context is to focus on increasing the purchasing capability of this segment without being exploited. Microfinance is the solution for it.

Earlier this segment was exploited by the village moneylenders whenever they needed loans. Historically, these people only took for the dire emergency or for agriculture machinery for tilling the land and women were even denied that also. Earlier, microfinancing was done by charitable institutions and at one point of time international development aid agencies and national governments made some efforts in developing countries.

But the real success of microfinance is that serving the poor has the same benefits as anywhere else. It attracts competition and creates an industry. "The poor are part of the definition of business. This has dramatic impact."

Philanthropy can be a victim of fashion, campaigns that rise and fall from time to time. Microfinance, on the other hand, sees the poor not as aid recipients but as clients. Aid recipients are passive and grateful; clients are active and demanding.

Though it is not the answer for everyone, not all enterprises merit a loan, and it is only one way in which a market has opened to serve the poor, its benefits are important to today's world. Microfinance may be a social safety net when no other social safety nets exist, which is the case in the vast majority of the world.

Microfinancing or giving tiny loans were/are considered an essential tool to lift the poor entrepreneur. 1970 was the start of Grameen (rural) Bank in Bangladesh by UNDP for microfinance for rural women. Government in India started rural bank (NABARD) for giving agriculture loans to farmers but the default rate is much higher and has not been a successful experiment.

Four emerging microfinance practices have been significant in helping the poor, low-income, rural, and women in this segment; and have been helpful in reducing the poverty and their economic helplessness to some extent. *The practice of microfinance has now changed for profit making by making the working model efficient and at the same time financing and helping the poor ruralites for more diverse products without any gender differentiation. This practice created more scope. The other significant practice that has emerged is that microfinance is not only available for the products for starting enterprises and buying technology and machinery for livelihood; but for the consumer goods also — both durable and non-durable for comforts of life and to improve their lifestyle.*

The third practice was the combined effect of these two and beneficial for businesses. The first two emerging practices created markets and increased the business volume for products and services targeted at them. The fourth practice that emerged as consequence of these was of utmost significance as this consumer segment is recognized as deserving the goods and services and right to comforts and improved lifestyles. They could buy TV, DVD for entertainment or could take loans to start or increase efficiency of an enterprise.

In India, self-help groups of companies like ICICI bank, the ITC e-Chaupal, the adult literacy program by TCS, and Shakti Initiative of HLL in India have realized the need to work their supply chain backward starting with the consumer expectations and experiences. For example, earlier, the bottom-of-the-pyramid persons have to depend on moneylenders. But ICICI and other banks saw these people as critical to its future. But how to convert them into customers in cost effective way? Initially, ICICI bank organized village self-help groups. These groups of 20 women are taught about saving, borrowing, investing and so on. Each woman contributes to the joint saving account with the other members of the group. Based on the self-help group's track record, the bank lends money to the group, which in turn lends money to the individual members. ICICI is working with local communities and NGOs to enlarge its reach.

The latest practice in microlending/microfinance is by profit microlenders. In developing country of India there are three such companies — SKS microfinance, Share Microfin Ltd., Bhartiya Samrudhi Finance who are in microfinancing business. They give tiny loans to the poor entrepreneurs in villages that help them to lift themselves up from the poverty rung.

SKS has changed the earlier standard model which was not efficient, had more overhead expenses and not making money. This model has its limits; poorly managed and unscalable. Now it follows the business model of McDonald or Starbucks using technology and standardized systems to bring efficiency. It made the model efficient. First, by streamlining the loan process system to deal with the borrowers; by organizing them to meet together in groups at appointed time and at one appointed place, to get the payments in pre-sorted denominations to save counting of soiled currency notes.

Second plan was to attract capital from big banking institutions. Now banks Citigroup, ABN AMRO, HSBC Holdings, ICICI banks are giving millions of dollars to SKS to lend out in India, since India has the potentialities. Once SKS has more than 100,000 borrowers with default rate 2 per cent they will be willing to invest. Moreover, foreign banks, under government pressure have to make 32 per cent of their loans to priority sectors including agriculture and rural industry. SKS put forth the argument, pay SKS to find borrowers and manage loans for you and you will get backdoor access to Indian consumer market. Thus microfinance is being taken beyond philanthropy.

Thirdly, to use simple loan management software that reduce the accounting time from hours to minutes. The software also helped to diversify the risks from giving loans for buffalo purchase only to tractor repair, setting up tea shops, or tyre re-treading, etc. Now SKS is hopeful about this model's efficiency and utility. It plans to bring health and crop insurance to the poor. It hopes to use Visa card technology to make micro loans as simple as getting cash from an ATM.

Thus, entrepreneurs get big banks to back small loans. ICICI bank in India plans microfinance and sell insurance also to them. India's Central Bank is so optimistic about this model that recently it changed its regulations to allow small rural organizations to act as agents for banks.

This program had its social resistance also. In 2004, SKS refusal to bribe local goons in the town of Nizamabad in Andhra Pradesh led to tough conflicts. Men with broken bottles and machetes attacked the loan officers and stole their cash. When SKS still refused to pay, it spread the rumors, that SKS was a Christian organization trying to convert Muslims. When local clerics heard the rumor they issued fatwa or religious ruling that loans cannot be taken from SKS. It has to pull out from the area and lose substantially, (News item May 2006).

A snapshot of microfinance activities of few rural banks in India is given in the Appendix 2. These banks design products of savings, credit, marketing of their members' products and microhealth insurance according to the needs of rural poor women population. These were the earlier practices in microfinance; and these do exist in parallel to the changing microfinance practices.

As micro credit gathers force; there is now hope that micro finance can be a large scale poverty alleviation tool. Banks too are shedding their old reluctance to lend to the poor, and are looking to tap the expertise of micro credit groups to create a new market.

The emerging practices are microfinance by profit micro-lenders, national and private banks and through private-public partnerships. Some of the profit microlender companies may be even foreign companies operating for developing countries. Moreover, providing the microfinance does not make any gender differentiations and covers both male and females; and both rural and urban poor.

The year 2006, the International Year of Microcredit, is a time to recognize that microfinance can help empower those with little or no access to traditional financial institutions.

Finance & Investments

Government is telling its people, we do not borrow global funds – we invite global businesses to invest.

The flow of funds globally, flow of talents and skills globally, and flow of businesses globally cannot only interconnect economy but boost economy worldwide.

Capital flow and investments globally is a must; and these global circulations of funds also gets into interdependency loop and get affected by the international factors. The investments of global funds in domestic economy create mutual economic benefits for its people and the foreign investors. Financial moves are driven by geopolitical events and also by global economic concerns and market stability or volatility. Since the next way the business products and services, and the finance inputs are handled globally even any next financial crisis will occur on a global scale. The global cues and the global factors affect the financial markets. The international economy and global financial markets require a continuing review of the representation, operations, and strategies. In the wake of changing global financial demands, trade and investments; the global financial institutions such as World Bank and IMF face challenges to restructure their strategies to meet the changing needs of developing countries in globalization investments and capital flow contexts. The convergence of communication technologies, political, and economic liberalization has transformed the way we live and communicate, trade and invest. A world connected by trade and technology must be connected by common values.

Earlier the developing nations were given aid by international organizations to boost their economies. This was borrowing money which they need to repay at one point of time. Moreover, it has its limitations and terms. How much and how many countries could borrow what they needed – they had no choice. The scenario has changed now. Different countries, different businesses and even individuals can choose where, with whom and in what segment they want to do business and on mutually beneficial terms. The interdependency of developed, developing and emerging markets is not for economic subjugation but for mutual economic benefits and prosperity. The best talents, best skills are in demand and sought for whichever country one may belong to. The flow of funds globally, flow of talents and skills globally, and flow of businesses globally can not only interconnect economy but boost economy worldwide.

Foreign direct investments (FDI) are done in three ways. These investments are done in manufacturing, infrastructures of roads, dams, bridges, flyovers metro rails, etc., on BOOT system (buy, own-operate and transfer). Second is investing in collaboration with businesses, acquisitions and mergers. These are stable and long-term investments. Third is short-term investment in stocks and bonds which are more liquid in nature.

Efficiency in economic management which can be instrumental for economic reforms and liberalization, planning strategies for direction and pace for economy, remedies for structural and resource backwardness and functional welfare model for all can impact achievement. This requires involved efforts of the governance and people.

The economic contexts of globalization highlight that global communication industries study ways of customizing or innovating products suitable within geo-linguistic or geo-political regions. The local level producers are drawn on the global codes and conventions. The information and entertainment products champion pre-dominantly the western ways of life, and values of capitalism and individualism. But there is exposure to different lifestyles of the world people. The enhanced and diversified trade and commerce markets usher countries into new economy. Unequal center and periphery relationships, hegemony versus rivalry, upper and lower class structures, and uneven cyclical developments affect world economy. The ideological categories and labels offer ideological self-satisfaction but impede and obscure the analysis of material real world, economic development, and real rather than ideal alternative choices it offers yesterday, today, and tomorrow.

There are three major trends that are shaping the future of the world. First, there is wide proliferation of the modern information and communication technologies. Second, there is increasing democratization of the social systems around the world. The third trend is the intensifying global expansion of mainly western-based corporations. *Thus the convergence of these trends — communication technologies, political, and economic liberalization has transformed the way we live and communicate, trade and invest.*

Global Investments are done by government, public, private partnerships in two ways: investment in people, and investment in infrastructure to boost economy of any country. Both kinds of investments need right kind of policies, political will, and flow of funds. *What is more challenging is that such investments do help the common person and are not beneficial for elite segment of the society only.*

In global economy and globalization contexts, investment in people is important. The focus is on creating more jobs and developing people's skills and talents to match the new jobs. This will create prosperity for people, lower unemployment and will alleviate poverty to some extent.

The expats in India have contributed immensely in setting up IT software and hardware initiatives in the country and setting BPO's through their innovative ideas and matching technology skills and investments. They have developed people's skills variously to match thus created jobs.

India has to open to foreign fund flow through foreign direct investments to create world class infrastructure in roads, bridges, flyovers, highways, airports, air travel, airlines, railroads, power, etc., not only to expand domestic economy but also to participate in global economy. Inviting global partnerships and global investments require world class basic infrastructure to let it function. Political stability and favorable economic policies, economic reforms and liberalization created credibility for the investors to invest in India. These foreign funds flow has facilitated India to create infrastructure needed for global partners to do business in India. On the other hand, the economic liberalization policies allowed Indian businesses to collaborate with global business partners to expand their businesses as well as tap the innovative trends in those businesses.

Such openness of global investments is expanding Indian economy and consumer facilities such as housing, healthcare, education, food, insurance, retail, transportation, tourism, etc. It is creating more and more jobs, higher incomes, higher consumerism and raising standards of living.

The more significant and crucial point for India, in this instance, and for other emerging markets also is that more jobs, higher incomes, higher consumerism and raising standards of living are created for majority of its population, not just the urban but rural populations also, for the lower income strata and for even the absolute poor. Such an endeavor calls for investments and finance spending for all segments of society.

India will invest the global finances to give better connectivity to people in all segments of society by providing good infrastructure. It makes efforts to give people quality of life by providing employment, higher income and availability of both basic and luxury affordable goods and services within the country.

This did need the change of stance and the changing communication practices of making people responsible for their own prosperity and not dependency on government. It needs collaborative efforts between the government and people. Here government is telling its people, we do not borrow global funds – we invite global businesses to invest in India. For this, we create credibility through the people of India who has to work hard, work diligently, with innovative ideas and skills which such partners may seek in us. The success lies in national public and private partnerships, global and national public and private partnerships. The result is better quality of life for you people. You can take it or leave it, the choice is yours, and the government is ready to guide you, support you with open and liberalized economic policies, transparency and accountability.

Reform seeks all-round change for the better. It is as much about empowering the politically disempowered as about enhancing integration with the global economy or enlarging the pool of people who can get a debt-swap right. In India (2006) the government has to put on hold disinvestment decisions of government held enterprises, the public state undertakings (PSU) in various economic sectors. Some of these are sick, some are non-profit-making and some are profit-making. But the fundamentals that the ruling government decided upon is that government should rule and not run the enterprises; let those be run by the businesses which are more suited to it. The other political parties in the coalition government oppose disinvestments on the premise of welfare model of employees. The economic community could see the decision as a set-back for the economic reforms.

Investments are done by foreign institutions and businesses in other countries including emerging markets of India, China, Brazil, and Russia, etc., for three reasons: i) because they find foreign markets profitable, ii) they acquire raw materials for their businesses from those foreign markets, and they acquire and merge the small foreign companies to expand their businesses. But percentage of foreign investment equity is regulated by concerned countries since they do not want foreign domination in the domestic companies and would protect the domestic economy. For example, in India, the foreign investment would be allowed more in certain sectors and less in others and no investments in certain sectors. Same way, certain sectors get open for business collaboration others are restricted. Government also regulates what kind and percentage of bonds and stocks investments can be made and in which specified foreign markets. These measures are taken to protect the interests of domestic enterprises and economy. Some countries like China may not regulate the foreign investments' quantum since all their economy depend on FDI and they match these with total exports.

Foreign funds have largely steered clear of politically volatile Pakistan; despite of its being strategic ally of US. The country remains a democracy with a military led government that faces threats from Al Qaeda-linked terror groups on its borders and insurgents. There is relatively little brokerage research done on Pakistani companies, making identification of investment targets tougher propositions. This is presumed to be not so safe market. Shahid Javed Burki (2006), a former top World Bank official warned of big current-account deficit, weak banks, and excessive speculative activity in its stock market.

Investment groups in globalization context consist of two groups. One group is involved in selling stocks and bond currencies, and in investment trading and selling. The other group is the multinationals which are directly involved in foreign investments, building factories around the world, striking long-term production deals or assembling of products in factories around the world.

Globalization is not primarily about trade and investment; it is about extending the range of opportunities people have for improving their lives from the few available in the immediate neighborhood to the multitude being created every moment around the world. *Trade and investment are mere means to that end.* But such expansion of the range of redeeming possibilities calls for something vital — people at large should have the ability both to recognize an opportunity when it pops up and to grab it. Creating that broad based capacity is part and parcel of reform. Education, health, infrastructure — these are obvious parts of the deal.

The markets around the world get under pressure due to rising oil prices and geopolitical tensions in the wake of North Korea's missile-tests, Middle East crisis of July 06, rising interest rates by US Federal bank, and other countries responding to it or being affected by it; and beside domestic political factors. The foreign funds investments thus follow a cautious approach.

The eruption of a new Middle East crisis, combined with bombings in India in July 06; and fears about Iran's nuclear ambitions swamp financial markets with risk just as they are adapting to a more uncertain economic climate. For the most part, though, this is likely to be a short-term scramble. Financial moves driven by geopolitical events have tended to reverse quite quickly over the past few years.

India's stock market recovered its poise and ended 3 per cent higher less than a day after fatal bomb explosions in the financial capital Mumbai. "Usually these things tend to calm down again," said Andreas Utermann, global chief investment officer of Allianz Global Investors, adding that the danger for investors is if some unexpected crisis hits and then deteriorates. Financial markets also tend to move quickly from one focus to another. A week ago (July 06), for example, Japan's Nikkei stock average fell as a series of missile tests by North Korea raised fears about security in Asia. But next, investors in Japan were fixated on something else entirely — whether the Bank of Japan was set to raise interest rates from zero for the first time in six years. The Bank of Japan statement is likely to have, at best, only marginal impact, as the liquidity from the Japanese market is expected to continue flowing towards emerging markets.

There are plenty of geopolitical worries on display for investors at the moment. Israel-Lebanon and Mumbai come on top of the North Korean missile tests, the tense diplomatic standoff between the West and Iran over the latter's nuclear program and ongoing trouble in Africa's oil-rich Niger delta. *What is significant for investors about such "event risks" this time is that they come when markets are generally jittery about the future already.* "You have a confluence of stuff at the same time," said Bob Parker, Vice Chairman of Credit Suisse's asset management arm. "You have got the market and economic factors ... and this geopolitical overlay."

Volatility swept through markets in May and June as uncertainty about the future shot up among global investors as it became apparent that the world was heading into an era of higher interest rates. The US Federal Reserve is poised for its 18th consecutive rise while the European Central Bank and Bank of Japan have also embarked on monetary tightening campaigns. The uncertainties are two-fold. First, the key integers in calculating the speed of global liquidity withdrawal are how high, and how rapidly interest rates are going to rise. Second is the impact of higher rates on economic growth. Some investors fear central bankers will overstretch, raising rates too high, stifling growth.

One result of this is that many investors have already taken risk off the table regardless of the surge in geopolitical pain. Increasing geopolitical tension will likely encourage more caution. At the very least, the geopolitical turmoil is expected to keep oil prices high enough that they threaten to take the bite out of consumer spending and feed the worries about a global economic slowdown.

The domestic markets will not be able to delink themselves from the global markets because of the global cues and the global factors. It is going to be a global market kind of leading where all other markets will go in the time to come.

Rakesh Mohan, Deputy Governor at the Reserve Bank of India (RBI), (July 06) commented that the impact of a freely floating exchange rate in developed countries is different for an emerging economy like India. So, RBI may opt to keep its grip over the rupee. The developed economies specialize in technology intensive products and the impact on the economy from exchange rate shifts is low. On the other hand, for the majority of developing countries which specialize in labor-intensive and low and intermediate technology products, profit margins are very thin. Consequently, exchange rate volatility has significant employment and output consequences. In the past 13 years, RBI has pursued a managed exchange rate policy without a fixed target. It intervenes when the rupee is over-or undervalued by more than 5 per cent on a trade-weighted index and if there are sharp fluctuations.

India bases monetary policy largely on domestic factors like growth and inflation, but outside events such as US interest rate changes are now playing a bigger role as the economy opens up. Analysts say with fuller convertibility, risks from volatile capital flows, particularly into high-yielding short-term debt, would rise. Unless the Central Bank keeps a hand on the currency, sharp fluctuations caused by rapid capital flows in and out of the country would impact interest rates.

"It remains to be seen whether financial market development in India can be such that this volatility does not result in unacceptable disruption in exchange rate determination and in domestic monetary conditions," Mohan said.

Global Banking: Business Strategy

In an era of globalization, a joint banking decision has to be taken in the event of financial crisis. Since the way the businesses products and services and the finance inputs are handled now; the next financial crisis will be on a global scale. This may require the concerted efforts of heads of major Central Banks of countries around the world involved (USA, Japan, China, UK, etc.) to keep the global economy on an even footing. *Therefore, the new communication practice is to have a head of Central Bank with deep knowledge of international economy, diplomatic skills to bring the fellow Central Bankers to the table for solutions and redress in case of crisis.*

In case of financial crisis, the small group of Central Banks should be able to prop up the global financial system. That approach requires a head that can collaborate effectively to defuse the financial crisis. The seventh G-20 meeting of Finance Ministers and Central Bank Governors in 2005 agreed to develop a roadmap to reform the World Bank and International Monetary Fund (IMF). However, the evolution of the international economy and global financial markets require a continuing review of the representation, operations, and strategies of World Bank and International Monetary Fund (IMF).

"We believe the IMF and the World Bank should work to enhance their institutional effectiveness, and that the strategic review needs to consider how to improve the internal governance," it noted. The statement said that these should adjust their operations in a timely manner so as to meet the changing needs of their members while maintaining their high-quality standards and results-orientation. Describing the G-20 statement on reforming these as a "breakthrough", Chinese Finance Minister Jin Renqing and Australian Treasurer Peter Costello said that such a step was required to meet the challenges posed to the IMF and the World Bank after 60 years of the establishment of those global financial institutions.

While welcoming the IMF Managing Director's 'Strategic Review' report, the meeting stressed that, "more work is needed to develop a roadmap for the future strategic reform, and we look forward to the work underway at the IMF to develop further details of the Strategic Review. All G-20 members are committed to ensuring the continued role of these institutions and will focus their efforts on strategic reform measures in the coming years".

The globalization of capital flow, foreign fund investments, and trade are likely to create mutual economic benefits for the participating countries, enhance their economic growth; and in the event of financial crisis there may be mutual support. These changed practices will not only create economic empowerment to specific countries but would result in global empowerment in general. The changing role of the International institutions would further enhance global empowerment to developing countries — not just by providing them financial aid to meet certain needs but providing them capital flow for partnerships to create economic growth.

Global Investment Climate

Asia's three giants China, India and Japan offer broad prospects for investors for business opportunities through their growth process. India has recently begun to take off as investment destination. It has advantages of Anglo-Saxon legal system and democracy and democratic institutions that allows for transparency such as media that exposes scandals, independent judges and legal system that provides some recourse. India has significantly younger population than China, in the next year; it should have 71 million new workers. India has a large number of world-class companies that are sophisticated and market driven. India does face challenges; its infrastructure needs improvement. It has difficult labor laws, regulatory inconsistencies and barriers to foreign investments in certain sectors. The fiscal deficit is too large and tariff rates are still high.

China needs to confront the social challenges of growth. Inequalities have been rising rapidly and there have been more social disturbances in 2004-05 as compared to earlier years. China will certainly grow dynamically though there could be some crisis along the way.

Japanese economy is resurging but the demographics are against the growth. Japan's economic revival, greater efficiency, and waning of the debt crisis are all positives for the country.

There will be more reliance on the Middle East, Africa, and Latin America. We see this in energy diplomacy. Japan and the US have an important role to play both in exploiting the growth opportunities and in dealing with the problems in Asian region. The US and Japan need to avoid a negative cycle relation with China and capitalize on India's emerging opportunities.

Finally, we need to figure out how to cope with consequences of global growth. *The market mechanism is the most effective way to deal with these problems.*

With investments heavily concentrated in China; US has become greatly dependent on China's continued growth and its vulnerability to overexposure. There are viable alternatives for foreign investments currently being offered by the Japanese economic resurgence and underestimated opportunities in Indian powerhouse. This will break US reliance on China (Calder Kent 2006).

India can be a powerful case for foreign investments despite its inefficiencies in certain industries. There is high level of technical education in India which has implications for investments and portfolio diversification. Investments may be made in information industries or service related sectors, insurance, financial, back office operations, legal frame works, etc. There are other Asian countries also with lot of potential such as Vietnam and Indonesia. Thailand and Malaysia have more advance economies than India. When we look at Asia we should look at the integrated, dynamic and marketized economies as total.

Summary

The flow of funds globally, flow of talents and skills globally, and flow of businesses globally cannot only interconnect economy but boost economy worldwide.

Capital flow and investments globally is must; and these global circulations of funds also gets into interdependency loop and get affected by the international factors.

Competition and innovations are important for managing business enterprises in globalization contexts. We need to rebuild a business culture with new global point of views. The significance lies in thinking globally and coping with global trends by capacity building and improved management techniques and facing changing challenges. Businesses are getting continually redefined, and reinventing new ways of doing business in the global market place is no longer an option – it is utter necessity. The essence of re-invention is innovation, invention and risk-taking in order to take the businesses to the next level of success. The external growth through partnerships, through M&A, strategic alliances, and creative deal-making is now an essential ingredient for continuously re-inventing any business. The globalization of businesses, of workplace, and how businesses in the future will be re-built and re-invented on global scale are top concerns of enterprises these days.

The companies doing global businesses must be staffed by international workforce. Any global model needs to be supported by outstanding local insights. They know the consumers better.

Businesses consistently ignore or underestimate the effects of local markets in fostering a global competitive advantage. In a modern skill-based economy the single most important element that drives a competitive industry is the existence of a demanding domestic market. Local market challenges increase competitive pressure on companies in that market, which then puts those companies in a better position to compete globally.

In today's global market-place, every company must think and perform like a world class competitor. In fast-changing global markets, companies have become more interdependent and strategic partnerships have become essential to build and maintain competitive strength. The primary motivations driving the globalization of the company are the comparative and competitive advantages that are gained by the integration of various value-added activities performed throughout the organization.

Business enterprises are developing new approaches and tools to fit in the evolving global competitive environment, and to make progress in terms of creating value as the pace of change accelerates.

Business innovation is not about services and products, it is about business models. Increasingly, large companies are also globalizing innovation as well. Innovation has changed, in 90s it involved dealing with vast technological shifts that disrupted and threatened companies. Today, it means building the process that promotes an idea generating culture. These innovative practices focus on merger and acquisition, business diversifications, enterprise architecture, restructuring corporate, low end markets, the poor, rural consumer segments, micro-financing, and disaster management.

In India, the recent changing business practices by enterprises are widening the scope of their businesses by diversifications. This has been possible because of changed practices about economic reforms, liberalization and opening of certain areas for foreign funding and equity as communicated by government policies and the businesses accepting the globalization challenges.

Trade and investment are means to extend the range of opportunities people have for improving their lives from the few available in the immediate neighborhood to the multitude being created every moment around the world. Global investments are done by government, public, private partnerships in two ways: investment in people, and investment in infrastructure to boost economy of any country. Inviting global partnerships and global investments require world class basic infrastructure to let it function. Political stability and favorable economic policies, economic reforms and liberalization created credibility for the investors to invest in India.

Decision-Making: Globalization

7

Decision-Making Process

Simple decisions and choices taken by individuals on a daily basis cumulatively have a global impact, and we need to break down global decisions into smaller frequent sustainability choices at the individual level.

A simple example of this process is to breakup a 'global' environmental problem such as desertification into individual causes. Deforestation, water extraction, agricultural practices affect the choices and decisions that influence causes such as lifestyle choices, consumption patterns, and technology development, etc. This may end up with one option that can be taken up at the local and individual level, such as, choice of the foods we eat (Hari Srinivas 2006).

The Decision-Making Pyramid has the individual level at the bottom level, and the global level at the top. In between are aligned other levels of decision-making: a community, city, and nation. While the bottom reflects simple decisions taken everyday, the top represents complex decisions taken more infrequently. Activities at the local/micro level influence the global level; and activities at the global level influence the local/micro level.

The pyramid is actually a continuum: as we go from the bottom to the top, we observe that individual decisions are replaced by decisions taken by groups. At the topmost, decisions become more complex covering a broader range of different aspects; quality and quantity of information required for decision-making increases; and short-term decisions are replaced by long-term decisions. The link between the top and the bottom of the sections of the pyramid is in fact cyclical: the everyday choices and preferences at the bottom of the pyramid influences policies developed at the global level.

On the other hand, decisions and agreements made at the global level clearly influence action at the bottom of the pyramid. Thus, outputs generated at the top of the pyramid, i.e. at the global level are policies oriented and have indirect impact on everyday life, while outputs generated at the bottom of the pyramid, i.e. at the individual level are action-oriented and have direct impact on everyday life.

The key message of the decision pyramid and decision-making process is i) we need to ensure that global goals and objectives are translated to viable local actions that cumulatively help achieve the objectives; ii) appropriate stakeholders should be involved at the right level, and partner with each other for the purpose of taking the right action at that level; and iii) proper communication among stakeholders—between levels and within a particular level is very important.

Decision-Making Practices

The decision-making practices have changed for participating in globalization and its related issues. *Right kind of decision-making is implied for global empowerment.* We focus on areas which are important and significant. The decision to participate in globalization, and go global is first and foremost. Under this broad umbrella are involved a bunch of decisions for framing economic policies, economic reforms and liberalization, to open markets, to use technology both personal and business, to encourage technological innovations both indigenous and external and decision making for investments and disinvestments. Equally important and significant are good governance and public administration practices to implement the decisions and public participation in decision-making about them.

As we observe, initially it may be conscious decision of the government and people to participate in globalization, and go global; but the pace of globalization is so fast and scope is getting wider so quickly that government and people have no choice but to be swayed by these waves. Participants soon realized, if they do not take quick decision, they will lag in the race and progress.

But the conscious and informed decision can be selective about the areas of operation such as outsourcing in its different formats, trade, business collaboration for setting up technology or other industries.

In this context government, enterprises and people are involved in different magnitude according to the role assigned by its political system. Thus it will differ in developed countries, developing countries with emerging markets, and underdeveloped countries. It will differ according to the market strengths, human capabilities and economy of the countries.

We identify governance, political leaders, enterprises, civil society and common public of a country as participating members in decision-making. The participating members of a country will interact with participating members of other countries to take in-formed decisions.

Salient Decision-Making Issues

Let us analyze how the decisions are taken at different levels of the decision-making pyramid and through the decision-making process in context of six important and significant interrelated issues to participate in globalization, economic policies and reforms, personal technology and business technology involvement, development of infrastructure to go global, and finance and investments. We analyze how governance, political will and public administration practices facilitate the decision-making for first five issues.

First salient issue: Participate in globalization and go global

We apply the decision making to the first issue of 'to participate in globalization, and go global'. Who makes decisions regarding globalization? We start with the goal: 'globalization participation'. We then analyze how this global goal impacts other levels and generate action, initiated and carried out by multi-stakeholder partnerships.

Level 1: Global

Actions and implications take place at global level: At this level, much attention is paid to trends in globalization, how trans-national trade and other globalization processes are increasing participation, and build scenarios on what will be the long-term impact of going global. Causes and effects are also outlined, with targets and plans of action for national governments.

Stakeholders involved are National enterprises, Multinationals, National and International governments, Universities and Research institutions, and International NGOs.

Level 2: National

Actions and implications take place at national level: The commitment that national governments participate in globalization and go global is converted into national economic policies and programs where support and guidance, in the form of rules, regulations legislation, research and development, financial support, etc., is outlined and implemented.

Stakeholders involved are National government ministries, agencies and departments; Research and Training institutions; Universities; Business and Industry associations such as Chambers of Commerce and Confederation of Industries.

Level 3: City

Actions and implications take place at this level: Cities and local governments take advantage of the special arrangements made at the national level to implement it locally, by integrating the goals and objectives within their own enterprise management plans. Local ordinances, regulations, etc., are combined with information campaigns and other means of informing the local communities of the need to go global. Campaigns can include special subsidies for developers, transportation planning, guidelines and checklists, etc. Many cities have now kept such goals at the center of their plans.

Stakeholders involved are local government agencies and departments, business and industry associations, local chambers of commerce, financial institutions, NGOs and community groups, local Universities and Research Institutions, etc.

Level 4: Community, Civil society, People

Local government and agencies, local NGO's involve local communities and civil society in dialogues and public debates through organized associations, such as resident associations, community focus groups and professional organizations to be apprised of local issues, problems, and positive and negative consequences and challenges that would entail of going global, glocal and participating in globalization. These may be job skills and training required to fit in the expanding markets; or the local enterprises small or big with conventional or update evolving products and services to foray into global markets and the ensuing development of consumer markets both domestic and global. The need for local physical infrastructure—such as roads and highways, modes of transport, etc., the human factor and social acceptance, business, and financial factors to make globalization viable.

The civil society comprising of professionals and supposedly well informed citizens would facilitate understanding of why we should participate in globalization and the need for efforts to put in by them and by the community and people. Efforts and decisions of people in general, however small, form the core for group decisions of community and civil society.

Actions and implications at this level are that it is imperative for people, communities and civil society to cooperate, collaborate and give feedback on local government and local agencies, and NGO's efforts for globalization participation.

This is the critical step where the guidelines, checklists, and regulations are converted to planning for globalism, glocalization, and globulation at the individual level that help in globalization.

Stakeholders involved are local government agencies and departments, local business and industry associations, local chambers of commerce, financial institutions, local NGOs and, local Universities and Research Institutions, etc., community groups, civil society and individuals in general.

The above cycle can be analyzed in reverse where the issue for global participation is stimulated or activated from people, communities and civil society who are at level 4 at the bottom in the decision-making pyramid. Their interest may be activated by media and other international exposure for better economic opportunities, improved lifestyles and consumer markets.

Media Role is significant in creating an ambiance for globalization and activating interest for globalization participation for better economic opportunities, improved life- styles and consumer markets. Globalization demands wider, instant connectivity with its global players; and various media channels provide it. Information is basic and essential component for globalization. Information is about products, ideas and services from around the world from the tiniest village to the metros in big and small countries. Flow of such information is provided ubiquitously by media channels. It facilitates the process of decision-making to go global, and to participate in globalization through globulation, glocalization and globalism. It also facilitates and guides the decisions of the global participants and players as the appropriate time and modes for participation. Media does provide feedbacks about the factors affecting these and the trends in globalization whether it is foreign funds investments, raising interest rates by governments, controlling inflation or need to outsource particular facilities. It would apprise the global participants of political and economic stability of a country, of local issues, problems, cultural practices and positive and negative consequences and challenges that would entail of going global. Both national and international media channels are involved with strong support of interpersonal communication channels.

Second salient issue: Economic policies

Economic policies would focus on economic growth, raising per capita income for its population, improved lifestyle, overall economic prosperity and development. Once we decide to participate in globalization, and go global; the participating members focus on the second issue of 'economic policies' conducive to participate in globalization and go global.

Actions and implications: In this context four points need consideration, i) economic policies conducive to do business globally, ii) economic policies focus on particular areas which are countries' strength such as India focusing on IT software, and BPOs in many areas, iii) joint ventures through collaborative models, and iv) expanding entrepreneurial activities abroad.

Expanding entrepreneurial activities abroad can be done in different ways: such as in India, Aditya Birla group expanding to Australian mines, or Tata expanding to south Africa, or Infosys technologies and TCS expanding its activities to USA, China and other countries. These business conglomerates use their finances and investments, and expertise with local physical and human resources. This form of globalization helps the economy of South Africa, China, USA and other countries and develops its people. The business as such will generate profits for the Birla, Tata, Infosys technologies and TCS. But what is needed is the liberalization of economic polices of India to let these people invest finances, and expertise in other countries and at the same time pool back the profits, import the appropriate technologies to India to further expand their businesses and benefit the Indian economy and Indian people.

Same way IBM and Microsoft would manufacture inexpensive and befitting PCs for rural areas in India. Motorola and Nokia would manufacture cellphones for Indian markets. As Indian cellphones are fast expanding at the lower socio-eco levels of the population as a necessity, they may focus on affordable cellphone for this level. It is a kind of interdependent circular loop of globalization participation benefiting both the partners and both are necessary parties for the deal to succeed. At this point India's economic policies should be liberalized to accept the foreign equity and ensuing benefits.

Three types of entrepreneurs would participate: big multinationals, joint ventures with two or multi-countries entrepreneurs/conglomerates, small groups and even individuals participating in different economic and commercial activities for economic benefits.

The economic policies of India in these contexts would need both national and international economic reforms and liberalization both for domestic and global players', to open markets for other countries; and to play on its strengths and identify and develop weaknesses and capabilities.

Thus, what is imperative in this context is: i) liberalization of economic policies and economic reforms, ii) open markets so that there are low import restrictions of products and services and finances and investments, iii) export of technology, expertise and foreign investments and finances are allowed, iv) India would need bureaucratic reforms to handle economic reforms suggesting hassle free, transparent dealings in setting up as well as winding up foreign businesses and free flow of businesses, and v) Favorable and conducive taxation policies and for repatriation of profits and investments.

Media role is important in creating awareness, information about economic policies for globalization participation; need for such policies, the stakeholders involved for planning such policies and the impact of such policies both positive and negative. More significant is projecting the feedback from people, civil society, entrepreneurs, international community on economic policies issues to the concerned stakeholders for further action. Thus, media contribute significantly in decision-making for economic policies.

Stakeholders

National governments, and international host countries, economists, technologists, communication specialists, and policy planners in these expertise areas are the stakeholders for actions and implementations. Entrepreneurial activities involve multinational, big and small enterprises, human resources of community groups, and individuals.

Third salient issue: Finance and Investments

Decision-making for finance and investments is corollary to economic policies. The focus is on capital investments, and human capital investments in global contexts and in global markets. How they are regulated in the interest of local, national, and international economy. How the national factors influence it and its international ramifications is important for globalization participation. Who are the main decision-makers in these contexts?

The focus of decision-making is: Does the participating country has adequate physical, financial and human resources to liberalize economic policies and invite global players and also let its people participate in globalization process with those global players? If not, how it intends to develop physical resources such as oil and gas dredging, setting oil refineries, and setting steel plants or even at the lowest rung — setting BPOs and telecommunication centers . The country may invite foreign entrepreneurs to invest their financial and other physical resources, as well as their expertise to set up such industries. This may be facilitated by collaborative or cooperative business models. The country may encourage the domestic industrialists by allowing them to import relevant technology, finances and expertise — all of them or either of them. Liberal economic policies with certain world class economic reforms, opening up of markets will be necessary for such an endeavor.

The decisions have to be made for financing other physical resources of infrastructure such as roads, highways, bridges, road transportation, railway, airport, ports, power, water and land to set up these facilities as world class facilities. These may be built through foreign funding as joint venture or by total foreign investments on BOT (buy-operate-transfer) basis depending on again country's openness of economic policies let the foreign capital flow in without reservations and restrictions or it may levy certain conditions.

Finances and investments are needed for developing human resources tó match the demands of globalization for manpower needs through expanding and upgrading education system and skills training. Development of local human resource is of utmost importance for glocalization. The domestic finances may be provided by government, private enterprises and institutions, universities and academic foundations. Foreign funding may be invested by such foreign counterparts.

Other preferred channels of capital investments by foreign investors may be the stock markets and bonds. Many international investors are investing in the emerging markets of India, China, etc. Both the parties gain. The flow of foreign funds in the stock markets boost the economy of the emerging markets as well as the international investors make profits also from stable and boosted economy.

Stakeholders involved in action and implementation in decision-making to finance and invest for different heads are national government through its bureaucracy channels, multinational and national enterprises and other associated businesses; both national and international universities and academic foundations; and civil society community groups and individuals.

As we discussed earlier in managing enterprises Chapter 6; global investments are done by government, public, and private partnerships in two ways: investment in people, and investment in infrastructure to boost economy of any country. Inviting global partnerships and global investments require world class basic infrastructure to let it function. Political stability and favorable economic policies, economic reforms and liberalization created credibility for the investors to invest in India.

All stake holders will be involved in decision-making in global contexts through the process of globulation, glocalization and globalism.

Media role is important to inform the participating parties about the political and financial stability of the country A where the other country B is going to invest. Who are other countries investing in country A. Since investments of others will also indirectly influence ROI (return of investments) of country B. What direct gain country B will get if it invests in upgrading people's skills or upgrading the infrastructure of telcom, roads, ports, etc. Media channels, either of country A or B or other countries may even caution about the bureaucratic hassles and corrupt practices of doing business in country A. This provides scenario to country B about the feasibility of investing in country A. Both national and international media set an agenda to inform, discuss, give feedback and guide the participants.

Fourth salient issue: Development of infrastructure to go global

World-class infrastructure has emerged as a fuel to power long-term and sustainable growth of economies, especially emerging economies, which are witnessing faster growth in demand for infrastructure and construction services. As far as the Indian economy is concerned, while the populace have been deprived of even a decent infrastructure set-up (due to government's slackness), what we are witnessing now is a kind of a revolution as far as the changes taking place in the industry are concerned.

Stakeholders involved in action and implementation. Who are the decision-makers to go for development of infrastructure? It could be country 'A' that invites other countries to do business with it. Other countries may be willing to do business with 'A' if there is appropriate world-class infrastructure as that would facilitate progress of their businesses; otherwise they may look for country 'C' who has or is willing to provide such infrastructural facilities. Therefore, government and enterprises of country 'A' would make-decisions about development of infrastructure to meet the needs of countries doing business with them. The decisions have to be made for developing physical resources of infrastructure such as roads, highways, bridges, road transportation, railway, airport, ports, power, water and land to set up these facilities as world class facilities and also developing human resources infrastructure to match the demands of globalization for manpower needs through expanding and upgrading education system and skills training. Development of local human resource is of utmost importance for glocalization. For example, IT skilled and English speaking human resources of India have attracted other countries to do business with it in comparison to China; whereas, China developed its physical infrastructure faster than India and captured more business on account of that.

The second scenario is when country 'B' does want to do business with 'A' because of low cost factor and it develops some of the infrastructure — physical or human for business profitability. Country "B' takes this decision in coordination with country 'A'.

What are the modes of development of infrastructure? Finances and investments are needed to develop these. These may be built through foreign funding as joint venture or by total foreign investments on BOT (buy-operate-transfer) basis depending again on openness of country's economic policies. Whether it would let the foreign capital flow in without reservations and restrictions or it may levy certain conditions. The other modes could be the foreign investments, public-private investments, collaborative investments of domestic private enterprises and foreign business enterprises as approved by the government. Human resource development is important component of doing business and investment in it both by country 'A' and 'B' and is essentially treated as part of business recurring expenses and investments for good ROI.

Stakeholders involved are participating governments, domestic private enterprises and foreign business enterprises.

Media highlights the need for world-class physical and human infrastructure to compete for global businesses. It also points the gaps in these infrastructures. Media channels reports. success stories about countries with developed physical infrastructure and their efforts in developing the human resource infrastructures through new educational models, skill development and training programs focusing on emerging practices. Both national and international media channels are actively involved.

Fifth salient issue: Decision-making for Technology involvement

This involvement includes personal technology, business technology for all the above-mentioned issues facilitating globalization participation, economic policies and reforms, the development of infrastructure to go global, and finance and capital investments. This will involve use, manufacture, import, marketing, innovation and innovative uses of personal technology and business technology.

Let us analyze who are the decision-makers in this context. The stakeholders who would equally dominate the decision-making process in these contexts would be technologists and IT centric industries both national and international. This would need support from national governments for policy regulations and rules. Both national and international associated businesses would support these decisions for using business technologies to upgrade their performance to world-class standards and for finance and investments. They would also bring efficiency to their businesses by use of personal technologies in their office set-ups.

Equally important would be the people who are the end users for personal technologies and benefit more when businesses use the upgraded technologies. Of course we cannot deny the role played by innovators of both business and personal technologies who take the decisions to upgrade, introduce new features in the existing technologies or entirely new according to the market demands of particular country market segments such as Nokia may bring affordable set of cellphone for the low socio-eco people of India who are the major consumers of cellphone.

Media facilitate decision-making in three ways: It highlights the upgraded and innovative technologies. It creates awareness and information about them. Earlier, media would report assessment of users' needs, and demands for such technologies. Now, it makes efforts to match the two, and facilitate decision-making as to which technologies are appropriate to use, in which technologies to invest; in and in what mode – to produce indigenously in collaboration with foreign stakeholders, or to invest its own resources in producing it, to import or transfer the technology.

Sixth salient issue: Governance, Political Will and Public Administration vis-à-vis globalization participation

The role of good governance, political leaders and public administration for good decision making is conducive to globalization progress, economic growth, protecting domestic businesses and economy and security; this is of utmost importance. How these are handled facilitate the success of country's participation in the globalization.

The stakeholders are: i) ruling government party and opposition political parties, political leaders and political activists, ii) administrators, economists, technology experts, technocrats, development experts and functionaries, iii) policy planners and policy makers, expert committees and researchers, and iv) civil society.

We have noted that the decision-making practices have changed for participating in globalization and its related issues. Our discussions in Chapter 2 'Thinking Global' highlight the changing decision-making practices because of changing stances in globalization through its three rounds periods: 1st round of globalization: 1800-1920, 2nd round lasted 1945-1989, and 3rd round and the present globalization era 1990 onwards. We have gone through these three rounds of globalization from political, social and technology perspectives. The technology perspective with progress in technologies has set up the globalization of politics, social, economics and business practices and skills.

In the first round, there was flow of capital, trade and labor across borders. People and goods moved across borders. The decision-making was by the national and international governments. Therefore, there was the vulnerability of capital, trade and people movement because of their (government) decisions for their own interests and political powers. This era of global finance capitalism was broken by World War I, Great Depression and Russian revolution. This fractured the world both physically and ideologically.

In the second round; few powers such as USA and Russia dominated the political and economic scenario in the international system. Globalization was occurring but only among the two countries and their leaders. The individuals and small businesses were not participating. So these few powers were the decision-makers. Majority of the decisions were long-term.

The third round and the present globalization era are different in many respects. A greater number of population and countries are participating. The governments, people, companies are participating in economic, political, social, and technological activities. There is degree of intensity with which the world is tied together in a single market-place.

All stake holders will be involved in decision-making in global contexts through the process of globulation, glocalization and globalism. This practice is different from earlier rounds of globalization where either the dominant political leaders or dominant countries or only the high-end community groups or people would be involved in decision-making. But in the present globalization era all are equally important decision-makers to facilitate globalization. The role of none is less important than others.

So presently, there are multiple decision-makers for multiple dimensions and perspectives of globalization. The emerging practice is that decision-making has become more complex and active involvement of all the stakeholders at the five levels of the decision-making paradigm becomes absolutely essential for the success of particular globalization program.

The second emerging practice is that there are more short-term than long-term decisions because of the fast pace of change in the globalization, globalism and glocal dimensions and the participating stakeholders accordingly. The focus of the decision-making also changes fast to keep pace. This impacts the process of decision-making and adds complexity.

Present globalization system has replaced cold war geopolitics as the defining force in world affairs today. In this era of globalization, we are all connected by Internet but nobody is in-charge and mutual interdependence for trade, finance, investments and economy, etc., is the driving force. This driving force and the quintessential symbols of connectivity have impacted the decision-making.

The defining anxiety in globalization is fear of rapid change from an enemy you cannot touch, feel or see — a sense that your life can be changed at any moment by anonymous economic and technological changes. This does impact the decision-making process.

Thus, what impacts the decision-making process in the present globalization era are the driving force of interdependency loop, the rapid change of decision-making focus, and the anxiety that life can be changed at any moment by anonymous economic and technological changes. The visibility, accountability and transparency of decision-making in various domains through both national and international media channels make us more vulnerable as well as cautious about the decisions we make; as it does not impact us alone but many players around us.

As we observe, the decision-making on these salient issues in globalization contexts will be a continuous process, these basic issues will dominate the scenario and others may get added. But what is likely to change is the agenda within these issues with changing times, changing demands of globalization, newer perspectives, emerging and upgraded technologies and likely changes in characteristics of human population and change in consumption and consumer patterns.

Summary

The everyday choices and preferences at the bottom of the pyramid (people) influences policies developed at the global level. On the other hand, decisions and agreements made at the global level clearly influence action at the bottom of the pyramid.

We identify governance, political leaders, enterprises, civil society and common public of a country as participating members in decision-making. The key message of the decision pyramid and decision-making process is that we need to ensure that global goals and objectives are translated to viable local actions that cumulatively help achieve the objectives.

There are few salient issues which are important and significant for decision-making in global contexts and for global empowerment. Decisions are taken at different levels of the decision-making pyramid and through the decision-making process in context of six salient, interrelated issues to participate in globalization, economic policies and reforms, personal technology and business technology involvement, development of infrastructure to go global, finance and investments; and governance, and public administration of the country vis-à-vis globalization participation.

The role of good governance, willingness and cooperation of political leaders and hassle free public administration practices for good decision-making is conducive to globalization progress, economic growth, protecting domestic businesses and economy and inviting investments and capital flow. Right kind of decision-making is implied for global empowerment.

Epilogue

8

Observations

Our discussions point that the democracy of information and information flow, communication technology as facilitator, technology context for businesses and various innovative technology updates, civil society organizations, private-and-public-sector, ICT products and services providers, pro-active ICT interventions in NGO sector, ICT platforms such as conferences, discussion forums and Universities; can contribute to global empowerment.

We expect enhanced global empowerment; when technology bridges the digital divide between developed and developing nations by interdependency loop; when technology, political and social will bridges the digital divide between various segments of society — rural and urban, between high and low socio-economic strata and between higher and lower educated. The later sets the stage for people empowerment which leads to enhanced global empowerment. Thus information, ICTs and various digital divide bridges and technology bridges contribute to global empowerment and enhance these experiences. 'The Technology Bridges' facilitate development and global empowerment.

Global empowerment does not mean political empowerment; but in current era, the empowerment comes from economic growth, economic prosperity, developing human resources and the development of society in general and for globalization roles. Thus, economic development and social development is equal to global empowerment. Secondly, it does not mean development of a single country; but it entails the development of all the partners and participants in the interdependency loop. Quite likely the development of these will vary. Thus, we cannot say 'Winner' country does the most for global empowerment through its achievements or even escalating conflicts, rather it is a term most appropriately used for all partners, participants in the interdependency loop. Even the countries on the periphery of the interdependency loop are likely to get both positive trickle down benefits and connectivity and negative trickle downs of tensions and conflicts.

The countries in the interdependency loop not only get involved in economic and social development but one way or the other they also get involved in conflicts, wars and tensions which become global issues through emerging political practices. Globalization should not have escalated political conflicts; rather it should have brought global peace; but the emerging political and religious practices and even business practices such as demand and supply issues of oil worldwide have different effects in creating global conflicts, wars, tensions and terrorism. This becomes more widespread and conflicts become global issues.

The practices are changing in different areas to fit the globalization roles. Countries and individuals are looking for best practices from around the world, learning lessons form experiences of those who have been practicing, learning skills to adopt or assimilate them. The overall effort is for global empowerment through these emerging practices. Thus, many new practices emerge continuously in contexts of globulation, glocalization, and globalism; and we endeavor to communicate our willingness to be in the globalization race through practicing them. The significant point is how these are communicated and what they are communicating.

(i) These practices are communicating a different amalgated business culture to its stakeholders. These relate to social, business, and techno-cultures.

(ii) How these changed practices are fitting in a country's social, business, political, economic, and cultural environments by assimilating the new practices with their earlier practices.

(iii) Globulation changes business disciplines and impact each other.

(iv) Glocalization, globalism practices create a different consumer profile for the youth by impact on employment, self-confidence, aspiration for higher standard of living. Higher disposable incomes and availability of new style of goods encourage consumerism. New styles of work such as in outsourcing centers in host countries create social issues as well biological problems.

(v) Consumer confidence is built by growth in economies, free and expanded markets.

The Future

Engardio (2006) argues that the multinationals from BRICS countries — Brazil, Russia, India, and China and even Egypt are coming on strong. They are hungry and want your customers. They are changing the global game. A new breed of multinationals is rising on the world scene, presenting both challenges and opportunities for established global players. There is shift in global empowerment through developing nations.

Boston consulting Group talks about the characteristics of the emerging-market companies that have the potential to reach the top of the global corporations. It identifies 100 such companies.

These companies establish primacy at home, expand in the neighboring countries, and then move to the West. Thus takes its brand to global in many different ways: (i) These target a niche market, focus on an industry, build scale and expand globally by acquiring smaller players. (ii) They tap ample low-cost talent at home, then develop innovative products, thus engineering to innovation. (iii) They take advantage of domestic oil, mineral or timber resources to attain a cost edge and then go global; they thus leverage the natural resources. (iv) They become a global player by buying oil and mineral reserves or partnering with other developing-nation companies by acquiring offshore asset. (v) They export a business model by sharpening a management system, and then replicate it globally through acquisitions.

What makes these upstart global contenders? Their key advantage is access to some of the world's most dynamic growth markets and immense pool of low-cost resources such as production workers, engineers, land, and petroleum or iron ore. But over and above the low cost factor are their innovativeness, expertly running businesses, cleverly and perceptively absorbing global consumer trends and technologies and getting new products to markets faster than their rivals.

These companies have learnt to make money by developing reliable, easy-to-use goods and services at very low prices and these skills have equipped them well for operating elsewhere in the world. By learning to compete, they have gained strength in development and marketing that helps them around the world. According to the World Bank estimates, from 1995 to 2003, corporate investment from one developing nation to another has more than tripled to $47 billion annually and probably neared now $60 billion since. That leaves the multinationals in strong position. *This legitimates the interdependency loop.*

The best of emerging multinationals though have amassed cash; they have also built global research and development networks and have world-class management.

Ram Charan (2006) points the shift in global empowerment through developing nations: (i) That emergence of world-class companies from developing nations. (ii) Emerging economies are no longer just about outsourcing or tapping into local markets but we are seeing the first wave of emerging-nation players that have clear advantage in their industries. (iii) The developing countries have entered into evolving game of multiple geographies rather than the commerce being dominated by 3-4 countries. The importance of this change poses challenge to the dominance of the West and Japan. *Thus seismic shift that began roughly 10 years back is brought by three forces: mobility of talent, mobility of capital and mobility of knowledge. Internet facilitated it.* Thus anyone from anywhere with determination can restructure a global industry. Example is Mittal industry. The rise of these multinationals was more than cheap labor and low currencies. Their leaders are good executors who see niches in the global economy and can tap world intellectual capital and financial markets to consolidate control across their industries.

In the interdependency loop, the mutual dependency is for gaining cooperation and collaboration. Being in the globalization arena has given some countries to choose partners independently and deal effectively with them. Therefore, at certain point, countries change the points in the loop to gain assertiveness and new relationship and wean dependency. Recently Venezuelan President Hugo Chavez deepened his relationship with China and signed several energy deals since Venezuela wants to reduce its dependency on sales of oil to the USA which is its biggest customer despite tense relations. At the same time China wants to diversify its reliance on Middle Eastern oil as it seeks to power its surging economy. In the future, we do expect such game-playing to boost globalization empowerment whether it is oil, steel, or nuclear power.

Niall Ferguson, Harvard Business professor in an interview (2005), identifies the major points that could lead to the decline of globalization. Though a crisis of globalization today is a low-probability and worst-case scenario. He observed the key causes could be: The over-stretch of the hegemonic empire of the United States. The escalation of rivalry between great powers such as the United States and China. The destabilization of the alliance system, i.e. the unreliability of the Europeans in American eyes, unreliability of the Americans in Japanese, South Korean, and Taiwanese eyes. The existence of a rogue regime sponsoring terror Syria, Iran, etc., and the rise of a revolutionary organization 'Al Qaeda' being hostile to global capitalism. The most significant actions or events that could accelerate or forestall another decline of globalization or swept into 'economic de-globalization' could be an international political crisis.

We expect globalization to enhance living standards. Economic and technological changes are likely to shrink effective distances still further in coming years, creating the potential for continued improvements in productivity, and living standards and for a reduction in global poverty.

The challenge for policy-makers is to ensure that the benefits of globalization are widely shared so that a consensus for welfare-enhancing change can be obtained. Though difficult, efforts to build a broad consensus for further globalization is worth making as the potential benefits of increased global economic integration are large indeed. Periodic global tensions and terrorism risks do threaten to constrain globalization but still globalization moves on.

In today's globalization system, it does not matter where you are, and who you are, but what matters the most is what you are, and on that depends the choices you make for prosperity in this system. This is likely to be true for the future of globalization with enhanced effects.

We have to engage in restless self-renewal because the sands of time are always shifting.

Appendices

APPENDIX 1

APDIP e-Notes are brief documents that present analyses of specific issues related to information and communication technologies (ICTs) for sustainable human development in the Asia-Pacific region. This series introduces readers to the who, what, where, why and how of a wide range of current issues related to ICTs such as e-governance, free and open source software, ICTs and poverty alleviation, Internet governance and many others.

- APDIP e-Note 1 — Voices from Asia Pacific: Internet governance for sustainable human development.
- APDIP e-Note 2 — Do Governments Actually Believe that ICT Can Help Alleviate Poverty? A perspective from Poverty Reduction Strategy Papers.

Digital Review of Asia Pacific offers comprehensive reports and useful analyses of how 29 economies/countries are using ICTs in business, government and civil society. The latest edition, 2005-2006, details developments and challenges facing the ICT industry in the Asia-Pacific region. It is an essential guide for ICT related policy development, planning, research and project implementation.

- e-Primers for the Information Economy, Society, and Polity Series introduces concepts, issues and trends surrounding the information economy. Titles include: e-Commerce and e-Business; e-Government; Genes, Technology and Policy; ICTs for Poverty Alleviation; ICT in Education; the Information Age; Legal and

Regulatory Issues; and Nets, Webs and the Information Infrastructure. Coming soon is one on Internet Governance.

- e-Primers on Free/Open Source Software (FOSS) Series serves as introductory documents to FOSS issues. Titles include: FOSS: A General Introduction; FOSS: Education; FOSS: Government Policy; and FOSS: Localization. A draft of the FOSS: Open Standards e-Primer is now available online for public review and feedback at: http://www.apdip.net/news/foss-open-standards-primer-draft.

UNDP-APDIP ICT4D Series seeks to provide concrete research and analysis on the strengths and weaknesses that are evident in ICT4D policies across the region. It focuses on applications of ICT policies and its impact in accelerating social and economic development.

CTO and ITU

The Commonwealth Telecommunication Organization (CTO), was created in 1901, and is an international development partnership between Commonwealth and non-Commonwealth governments, business and civil society organizations. It provides the international community with effective means to help bridge the digital divide and achieve social and economic development, by delivering to developing countries unique knowledge-sharing programs in the use of information and communication technologies (ICT) in the specific areas of telecommunications, IT, broadcasting and the Internet.

The International Events Division is fundamental to the CTO's aims of bridging the digital divide and achieving social and economic development. These events form the backbone of our knowledge-sharing programs in the use of information and communication technologies.

International Telecommunication Union (ITU) is the leading United Nations agency for information and communication technology issues, and the global focal point for governments and the private sector in developing networks and services. For more than 140 years, ITU has coordinated the shared global use of the radio spectrum, promoted international cooperation in assigning satellite orbits, worked to improve telecommunication infrastructure in the developing world, and established the worldwide standards that foster seamless interconnection of a vast range of communications systems.

ITU also organizes worldwide and regional exhibitions and forums bringing together the most influential representatives of government and the telecommunications industry to exchange ideas, knowledge and technology for the benefit of the global community, and in particular the developing world.

ICTs research and new communication practices

The need for new communication practices focus on certain ICTs research areas which eventually will deliver innovative communication practices for better use of ICTs in people's life-style, professions and businesses:

- Research and development into innovative ICT applications, with a clear focus on practical and replicable approaches and techniques.
- Research on Internet infrastructure design, performance, management policy and related topics.
- Research with clear learning outcomes and social impacts from specific ICT policies and interventions and application of Internet technologies.
- Research on policy matters affecting Internet networking in the Asia-Pacific region, especially linked to areas such as culture, environment, gender equity, health, social equity, sustainable community development, technology diffusion/transfer, and benefits to rural areas.
- Development of practical solutions based on the application of proven and readily available Internet technologies with minimum basic research.
- Technology related issues such as broadband connectivity, "last mile innovation, mobile and wireless

technologies for the developing world, and increasing the capacity or efficiency of existing network infrastructures.

APPENDIX 2

Microfinance

A snapshot of microfinance activities of few rural banks in India is listed.

1. Rural Women Bank

Mann Deshi Mahila Sah Bank Ltd., Mhaswad India

Sector of activity: Financial Services

Marketing, Agriculture.

This bank designs, products of savings, credit, and micro-health insurance according to the need of rural poor women population. (i) Savings: Bank has catered daily, weekly and monthly saving products for poor women. (ii) Credit: Bank has designed the credit program, which has the repaying system of daily, weekly and monthly. (iii) Micro health insurance: The Bank with partners has designed microinsurance products; because of these products poor communities in the areas are saved from the debt trap of money-lender. Primary clients are street vendors, milk vendors, shepherd women and nomadic women, craft workers and small entrepreneurs. (iv) Impact: Prior to Mann Deshi Mahila Bank, women in this area had no financial options other than taking emergency loans from moneylenders at exorbitant rate of interest. Now women take loans from the bank to start new businesses and to develop productive assets. If women control the finances, the entire family benefits as more money is spent on children, education, and household necessities.

The operational model: Bank has appointed agents giving door-to-door services of savings, lending. In return they get the commission. This makes the distribution services sustainable and viable. Agent is using wireless simputers, this helps daily compliance of data even from the remote areas (simputer is wireless small computer in which list of the clients and their saving can be saved and data can be transferred to computers).

Bank launched its marketing center for farmers and producers. Center is equipped with technology like cellphones and Internet which helps them to inquire about the market rate and get the better prices for their commodity. Bank lends umbrellas on a per day basis repayment at low interest rate to women who sell in open-air weekly markets. The umbrellas reduce women's risk of falling ill, which directly affects their ability to earn. One recurring difficulty faced by the clients is the inability to keep their account details confidential. Many of the clients do not store their passbooks in their home for fear of demands on their hard-earned or newly acquired loan money from their husbands. In response to this problem, the bank has provided Sim-cards through which women can deposit or withdraw their money. Daily data information is complied with the bank. Regular monthly meeting of SHG leader and quarterly meeting of co-coordinators help to get feedback and ideas about product.

Financial model: Bank was started with savings and share holdings of local population. It collects tiny savings from the village women and credit is given to the needy. Operational cost is met by the interest paid by needy and low-income women who take loans for small businesses. Bank also advocates local people to invest in saving and capital reserve, this helps to provide services to the needy and poor, other wise they will have to go to moneylender and pay exorbitant rate of interests. If women invest in the shares of the bank, they can get the dividend and avail the facility of marketing their products. This motivares them to invest in capital reserves.

2. In Kerala State, near India's southern tip, bureaucrats work with the poorest women in a program called Kudumbashree, or Family Prosperity. The aim is to identify the women's needs — from literacy and training to housing, health care and jobs — and to put them in-charge of managing their own development.

The women set up self-help savings groups, move on to microfinance and loans, and then establish their own micro-enterprises; the government helps them identify opportunities and gives them training in areas like information technology and marketing.

Thousands of enterprises have been established, from a data-processing company that has grown in two years to employ 20 people, to businesses offering beauty products, plumbing services, catering and garbage collection.

3. In Gujarat, even more ambitious schemes are being led by the *Self-Employed Women's Association*, a trade union, development organization and women's movement rolled up in one. The association runs a bank catering to the poorest women, champions the rights of the poorest workers, offers literacy classes and computer classes for teenagers, sponsors doctors in rural areas and organizes agricultural and textile cooperatives. It makes efforts to develop the entrepreneurial skills of the poorest in the face of global competition. To protect jobs, it analyzes global trends in fashion and then train them; and help market its members' textiles and products.

4. In Mumbai, a millionaire property developer, Mukesh Mehta, is the brains behind plans to transform Asia's largest slum, Dharavi. The goal is to build better housing through public-private partnerships and to upgrade the skills and equipment of the workers in Dharavi's cottage industries, from potters to leather workers, and to give them consultancy. The bold plan also aims to bring the rich into Dharavi without driving out the poor. The goal is to attract leading designers, doctors, cultural institutes and top schools, which in return for providing cheap or free services to the poor can use the facilities that are being built to provide much more expensive services to the rich.

If India can harness the vision and innovativeness of these curious bedfellows — from bureaucrats to women's trade union to millionaire property developer — then it may find a way to tackle poverty today, not in 20 years.

Bibliography

Albrow, M. and King, E., *Globalization, Knowledge, and Society.* Sage Publications, London, 1990.

Berg, Ann-Jorunn, *The Smart House* in Heap Nick, Ray Thomas et al. (eds.), *Information Technology and Society.* Sage Publications, London, 1995.

Bartlett, C. & Ghoushal, Sumantra, *Managing across Borders: The Transnational Solution,* 2nd edition. Harvard Business Press, 1999.

Beniger, J.R., *The Control Revolution: Technological and Economic Origins of the Information Society.* Harvard University Press, Cambridge, 1997.

BusinessWeek.com, 5/3/06 *AMD — sticks Intel.*

Calder, Kent, *Strategies for Business Portfolio Diversification in Asia.* Seminar, New York, June 2006.

Calder, Kent, *Asia's Political-Economic Transformation and Implications for US-Japan Relations.* Seminar, New York, June 2006.

Castells, M., *The Information Age : The Rise of the Network Society.* Blackwell, Oxford, 1995.

Cairncross, Francis, *The Death of Distance: How the Communication Revolution is Changing Our Lives.* Harvard Business School Press, 2001.

Charan, Ram, "Why it is a Small World After All," *Business Week,* July 31, 2006.

Christensen, Clayton, Interview with *Economic Times* in Bombay (2006).

Christopher, A., Bartlett and Ghoshal, Sumantra, *Companies, Cultures and the Transformation to the Transnational,* 1999.

Dunning, John (ed.), *Regions, Globalization and the Knowledge Based Economy.* Oxford University Press, 2002.

Dunning, John (ed.), *Making Globalization Good: The Moral Challenges of Global Capitalism.* Oxford University Press, 2004.

Dutton, William, H. (ed.), *Information and Communication Technologies: Visions and Realities*. Oxford University Press, New York, 1996.

The Economist. Canyon or Mirage, 22 January 2004.

The Economist. Calling an End to Poverty, 7 July 2005.

Economic Survey of Apex Economic Associations India (2005).

Edelweiss IT Report (2006).

Edge, David, *The Social Shaping of Technology* in Heap Nick, Ray Thomas et al. (eds.), *Information Technology and Society*. Sage Publications, London, 1995.

Engardio, Pete, "Emerging Giants." *Business Week*, July 31, 2006.

Forbes Global CEO Conferences, 2006, 2005.

Francisco, Dao, *Underestimating China's Market Advantage*. Executive Action No. 154, July 2005.

Francisco, Dao, *China: Creating an Unlikely Edge in the Global Market Share Battle*. Executive Action No. 154, July 2005.

Friedman, T.L., *The World is Flat: A Brief History of the Twenty-First Century*, 2005.

Fukuyama, Francis, "Our foreign Legions" *Wall Street Journal*, Jan. 26, 2004.

Garnick, Richard, Address in *8th Annual CEO Summit 2006*.

Gasmi, F. and Virto, L.R., *Telecommunications Technologies Deployment in Developing Countries — Role of Markets and Institutions*.

Ghoshal, Sumanta and Bartlett, Christopher, *Individualized Corporation*. Harper Perennial, 1999.

Hanna, Julia, "India Arrives on the Global Stage." *HBS Alumni Bulletin*, Vol. 82, No. 2, June 2006.

Henig, Peter and Lowe, Ken, Richard, Garnick, Address, in *8th Annual CEO Summit 2006*.

Harrison, Lawrence, E., et al. (ed.), *Culture Matters: How Values Shape Human Progress*. Basic Books, New York, 2001.

Held and Mcgrew, T. (eds.), *Modernity and its Futures*. Polity Press, Cambridge, 1992.

Hanson, J., Narula, Uma, *New Communication Technologies in Developing Countries*, Lawrence Erlbaum Associates, New Jersey, 1990.

Hagel, John and Seely, Brown, *The Only Sustainable Edge: Why Business Strategy Depends on Productive Friction and Dynamic Specialization*. Harvard Business School Press, 2005.

Heskett, James, L., *Has Globalization Reached Its Peak*. Harvard Business School Press, 2006.

Irving, I., *New Technologies Benefits All Nations* in Global issues On-line serial, Sept. 1996.

Jagdish, Bhagwatı, *In Defense of Globalization.* Oxford University Press, 2004.

Jackson, Harry and Normand, Frigon, *Achieving the Competitive Edge: A Practical Guide World-Class Competition.* John Wiley and Sons, 1996.

Josef Joffe review of the book *The Lexus and the Olive Tree* by Friedman Thomas 1999 Farrar, Straus & Giroux, New York.

Kelly and Littman, *Ten Faces of Innovations.* Currenecy/Doubleday, New York, 2005.

Lowe, Ken, *Information Technologies and International Development (ITID).* MIT Press Journal, 2006.

Liberthal, Kenneth and Prahlad, C.K., *The End of Corporate Imperialism.* Harvard Business Review, Aug. 2003, Vol. 81, 109-17.

Microsoft 2007 Office Preview Site, May 2006.

Mackay, Hughie, *Theorizing the IT Society Relationship* in Heap Nick, Ray Thomas et al. (eds.), *Information Technology and Society.* Sage Publications, London, 1995.

Malik, P. and de Silva, H., *Diversifying Network Particulars: A Study on India's Universal Service Instruments.* WDR Dialogue Theme 3rd Cycle Discussion, 2005.

Michie and Grieve, Smith, *Globalization, Growth, and Governance: Towards an Innovative Economy.* Oxford University Press, 2004.

Michie and Smith, Grieve, *Globalization and the Human Factor: Critical Insights.* Ashland Press, 2004.

Narula, Uma, *Second Thoughts on Development.* Unpublished paper, CNET, New Delhi, 1997.

Narula, Uma, "The Cultural Challenge of Communication Technology." *American Behavioural Scientist,* Vol. 32, No. 2, Nov-Dec. 1988, 194-207, Sage Publications, Newburyport, USA.

Narula, Uma and Pearce, W. (eds.), *Culture, Politics, and Research Programs.* Lawrence Erlbaum, New Jersey, 1990.

Narula, Uma, "Development Bureaucracy in India : Dilemmas Dependencies." *Perspectives in Development Communication.* Sage Publications, New Delhi, 1993.

Narula, Uma, *Communication Perspectives: Cultural Diffusion, Dynamics and Challenges.* HarAnand Publications, New Delhi, 2000.

Narula, Uma, *Media Communication Technologies: New Perspectives.* HarAnand Publications, New Delhi, 2001.

Narula, Uma, *Let Us Do It Ourselves.* Mimeo World Bank, 2000.

Narula, Uma, *Technology Revisited: India Case Study*. Mimeo, 2003.

Narula, Uma, *International Communication: Discourses*. Mimeo, 2003.

Narula, Uma, *Business Practices: Modern Trends*. Atlantic Publishers and Distributors (P) Ltd., New Delhi, 2006 b.

Narula, Uma, *Handbook of Communication Models, Perspectives, Strategies*. Atlantic Publishers and Distributors (P) Ltd., New Delhi, 2006 a.

Narula, Uma, *Dynamics of Mass Communications: Theory and Practice*. Atlantic Publishers and Distributors (P) Ltd., New Delhi, 2006 c.

Niall, Ferguson, Interview Report in *HBS Working Knowledge,* 2005.

Nilekani, CEO, Infosys, S. Annaswamy IBM, Davenport Thomas, quoted in News items *Economic Times,* New Delhi, May 2006.

Penman and Sless (1990, 233), "Public Domain in Australia" in Narula, Uma and Pearce, W. (eds.), *Culture, Politics and Research Programs*. Lawrence Erlbaum, New Jersey, 1990.

Porter, Michel, Research Harvard Business School, 2005

Prahlad, C.K., "Bringing Down the Digital Divide: How Mobile Communications will Underpin the Economic Uplift of the World's Aspiring Poor" in *Tax and the Digital Divide: How New Approaches to Mobile Taxation can Connect the Unconnected* 2005a.

Prahlad, C.K. *The Fortune at the Bottom of the Pyramid: Eradicating Poverty through Profit*. Wharton School Publishing, Upper Saddle River, New Jersey, 2004b.

Rao, Manmohan, *Digital Asia Pacific Review Reports,* 2002.

Robert, Cook, Philips, *The Winners-Take-All-Society*. Penguin, 1996.

Scherer, F.M., *New Perspectives on Economic Growth and Technological Innovations,* 1999.

Schoolnet Research, *Enhancing Human Capital Index: New Approaches for the Knowledge Economy*. Education background paper presented at the GIIC Conference, New Delhi, 14-15 March, 2002.

Schneider, S.C., "Information overload: causes and consequences," *Human Systems Management,* 7, 143-153.

Telecom Regulatory Authority of India, (2005). *The Indian Telecom Services: Performance Indicators, July–September 2005*. Retrieved February 1, 2006 from http://www.trai.gov.in/report27dec05part1.pdf

UNESCO (2003), *Information, Communication and Knowledge: Building Contemporary Societies.*

UNIDO, *The Competitive Edge.*

UNFPA report, "The Promise of Equality: Gender Equity, Reproductive Health and the Millennium Development Goals."

US Government White paper on Outsourcing and Offshoring (May 11, 2004).

Waverman, L., Meschi, M. and Fuss, M., *The Impact of Telecoms on Economic Growth in Developing Countries.* Report World Bank, 2006.

Websites: Intel.com, Wikipedia, Dictionary.com, TV guideline, Techtree.com India, World Bank report, *India and the Knowledge Economy: Leveraging Strengths and Opportunities,* June 28, 2005.

Wireless Networking in the Developing World. Online e-Book, June 2006.

Yoffee, *Competing in the Age of Digital Convergence, Competing on Internet Time, and Judo Strategy.* Harvard Business School Press, 2004.

Subject Index

A

B

C

D